STRATEGIC HOMELAND INTERVENTION ENFORCEMENT LOGISTICS DIVISION

FURY'S

STRATEGIC H

LOGIST

COLLECTION EDITOR JENNIFER GRÜNWALD ASSISTANT EDITORS ALEX STARBUCK & NELSON RIBEIRO EDITOR, SPECIAL PROJECTS MARK D. BEAZLEY SENIOR EDITOR, SPECIAL PROJECTS JEFF YOUNGQUIST

SENIOR VICE PRESIDENT OF SALES DAVID GABRIEL SVP OF BRAND PLANNING & COMMUNICATIONS MICHAEL PASCIULLO EDITOR IN CHIEF AXEL ALONSO CHIEF CREATIVE OFFICER JOE QUESADA PUBLISHER DAN BUCKLEY EXECUTIVE PRODUCER ALAN F

MARVEL'S THE AVENGERS PRELUDE: FURY'S BIG WEEK. Contains material originally published in magazine form as MARVEL'S THE AVENGERS PRELUDE: FURY'S BIG WEEK #1-4. First printing ISBN# 978-0-7851-6341-1. Published by MARVEL WORLDWIDE, INC., a subsidiary of MARVEL ENTERTAINMENT, LLC. OFFICE OF PUBLICATION: 135 West 50th Street, New York, NY 10020. Copyright © Marvel Characters, Inc. All rights reserved. $14.99 per copy in the U.S. and $16.99 in Canada (GST #R127032852); Canadian Agreement #40668537. All characters featured in this issue and the dis names and likenesses thereof, and all related indicia are trademarks of Marvel Characters, Inc. No similarity between any of the names, characters, persons, and/or institutions in this magazine with t any living or dead person or institution is intended, and any such similarity which may exist is purely coincidental. **Printed in the U.S.A.** ALAN FINE, EVP - Office of the President, Marvel Worldwide, EVP & CMO Marvel Characters B.V.; DAN BUCKLEY, Publisher & President - Print, Animation & Digital Divisions; JOE QUESADA, Chief Creative Officer; TOM BREVOORT, SVP of Publishing; DAVID BOGART Operations & Procurement, Publishing; RUWAN JAYATILLEKE, SVP & Associate Publisher, Publishing; C.B. CEBULSKI, SVP of Creator & Content Development; DAVID GABRIEL, SVP of Publishing Sales & Circ MICHAEL PASCIULLO, SVP of Brand Planning & Communications; JIM O'KEEFE, VP of Operations & Logistics; DAN CARR, Executive Director of Publishing Technology; SUSAN CRESPI, Editorial Ope Manager; ALEX MORALES, Publishing Operations Manager; STAN LEE, Chairman Emeritus. For information regarding advertising in Marvel Comics or on Marvel.com, please contact John Dokes, SVP Int Sales and Marketing, at jdokes@marvel.com. For Marvel subscription inquiries, please call 800-217-9158. **Manufactured between 3/29/2012 and 4/17/2012 by QUAD/GRAPHICS, DUBUQUE, I**

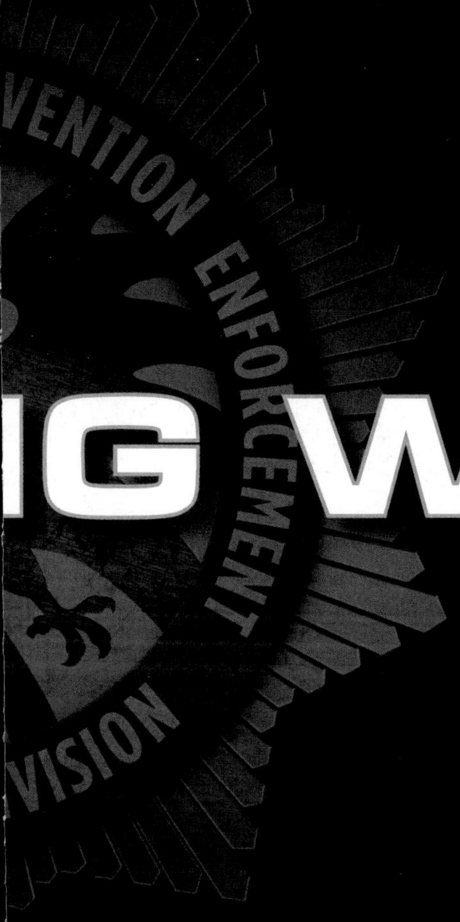
VENTION
ENFORCEMENT
VISION

IG WEEK

PLOT CHRISTOPHER YOST & ERIC PEARSON SCRIPT ERIC PEARSON

APTERS ONE & THREE ARTIST LUKE ROSS CHAPTERS TWO & FOUR PENCILER DANIEL HDR CHAPTERS TWO & FOUR INKER MARK PENNINGTON CHAPTERS FIVE & SEVEN PENCILER AGUSTIN PADILLA

CHAPTERS FIVE & SEVEN INKER DON HO CHAPTERS SIX & EIGHT PENCILER WELLINTON ALVES CHAPTERS SIX & EIGHT INKER RICK KETCHAM WITH DON HO

COLORIST CHRIS SOTOMAYOR LETTERER CHRIS ELIOPOLOUS WITH JOE CARAMAGNA

ASSISTANT EDITOR JON MOISAN EDITOR SANA AMANAT

MARVEL STUDIOS

CREATIVE MANAGER WILL CORONA PILGRIM DIRECTOR OF DEVELOPMENT BRAD WINDERBAUM CREATIVE EXECUTIVE JONATHAN SCHWARTZ

SVP PRODUCTION & DEVELOPMENT JEREMY LATCHAM PRESIDENT KEVIN FIEGE

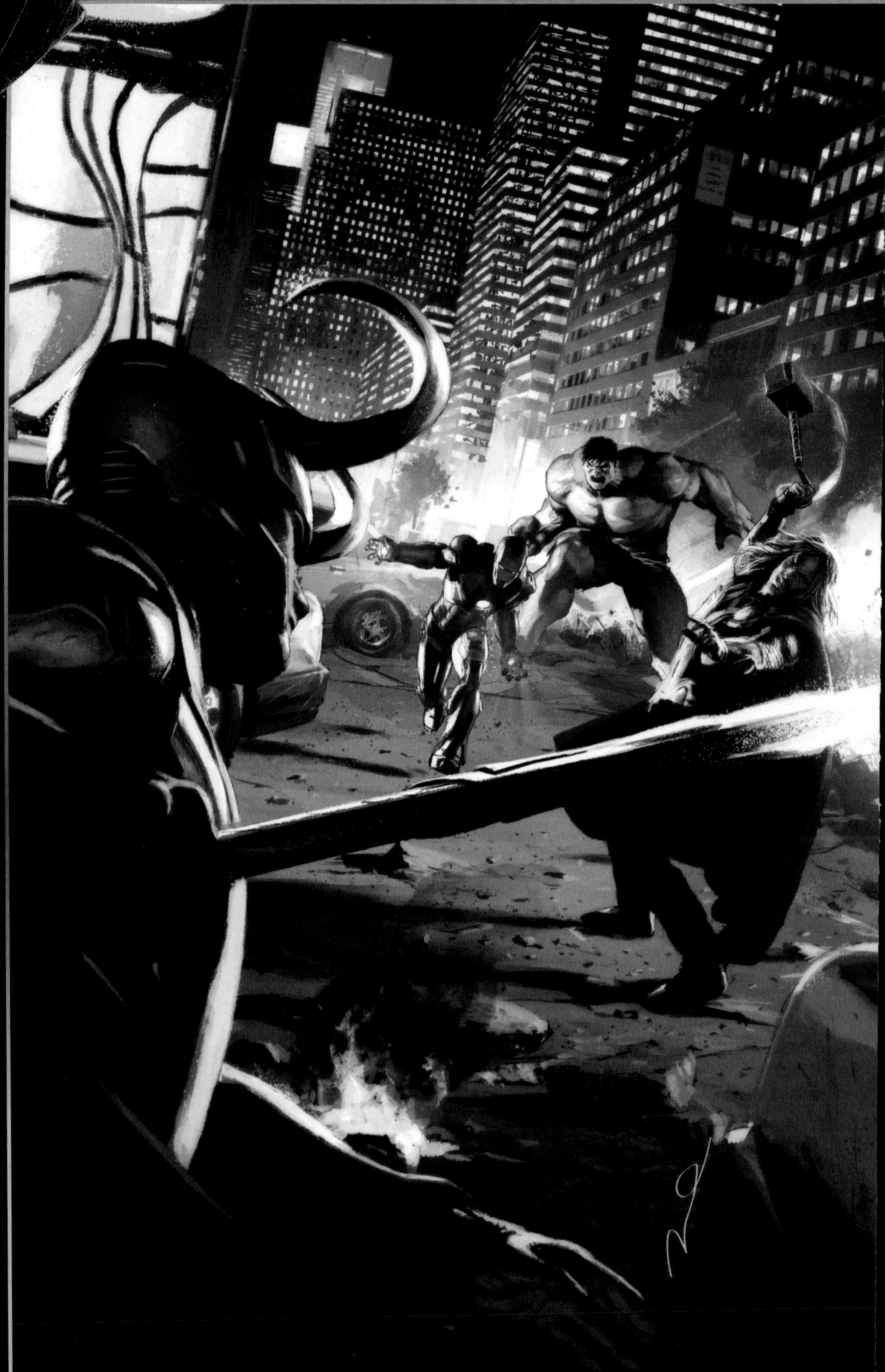

ONE

PROLOGUE

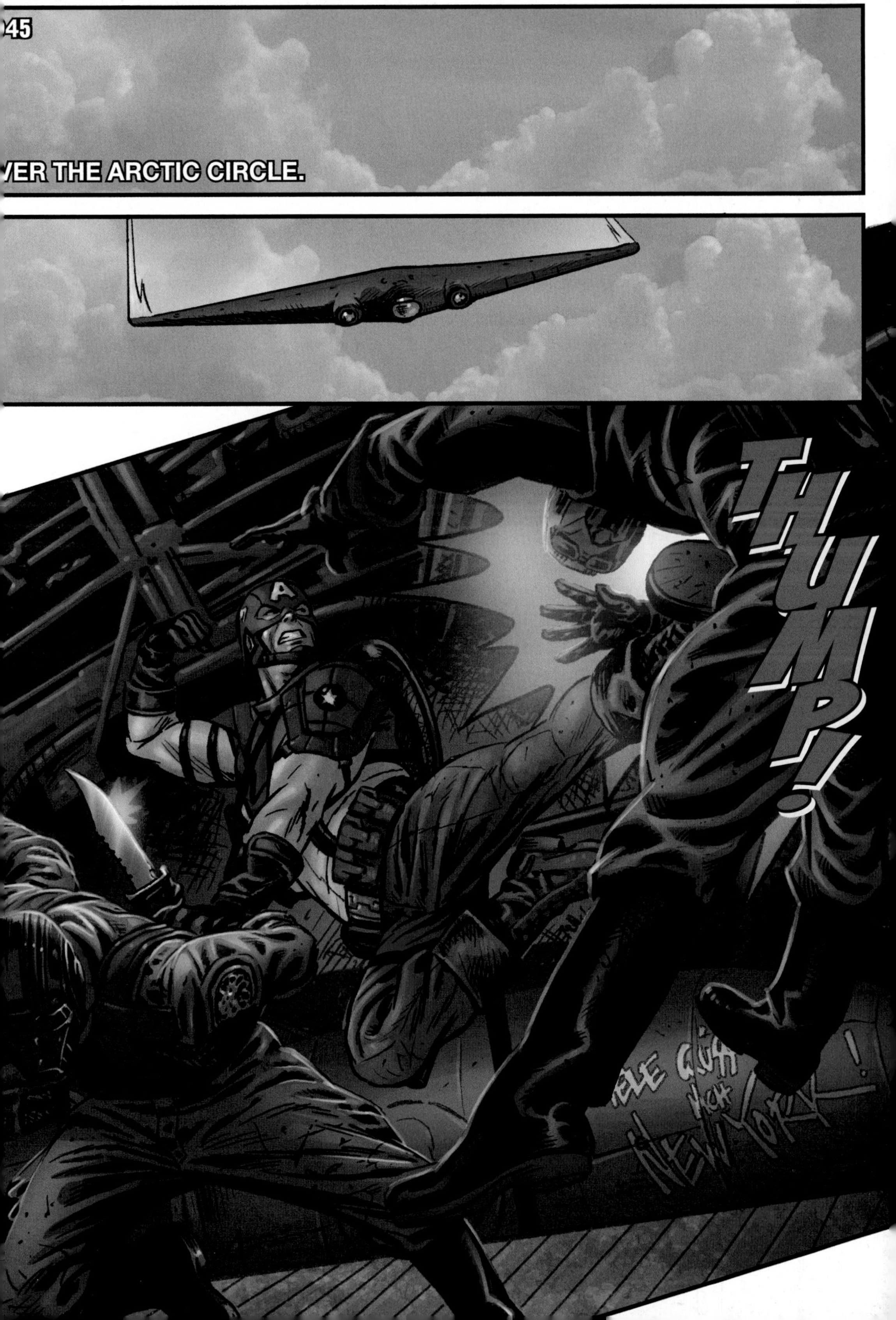
45
VER THE ARCTIC CIRCLE.
THUMP!

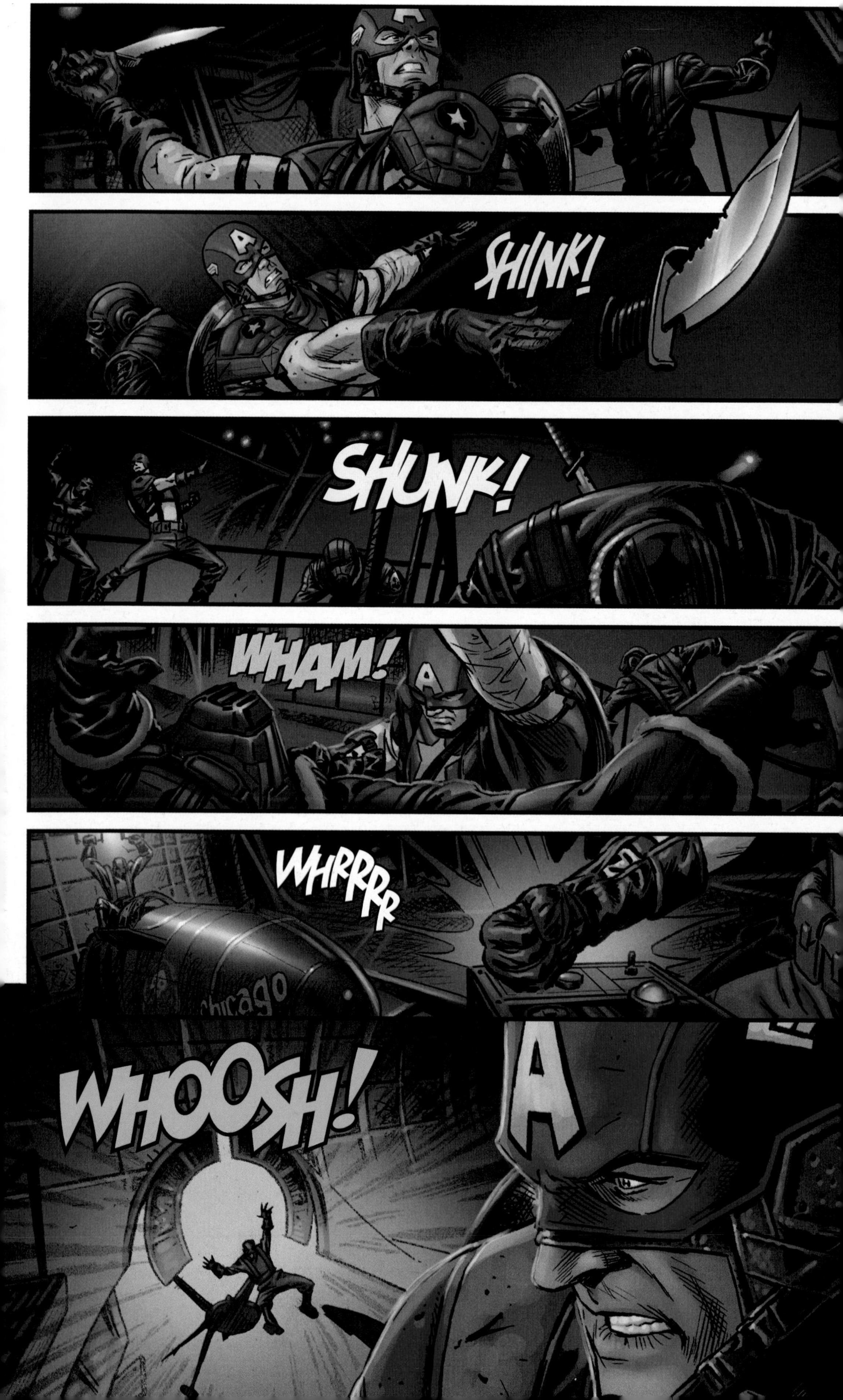
SHINK!
SHUNK!
WHAM!
WHRRRR
CHICAGO
WHOOSH!

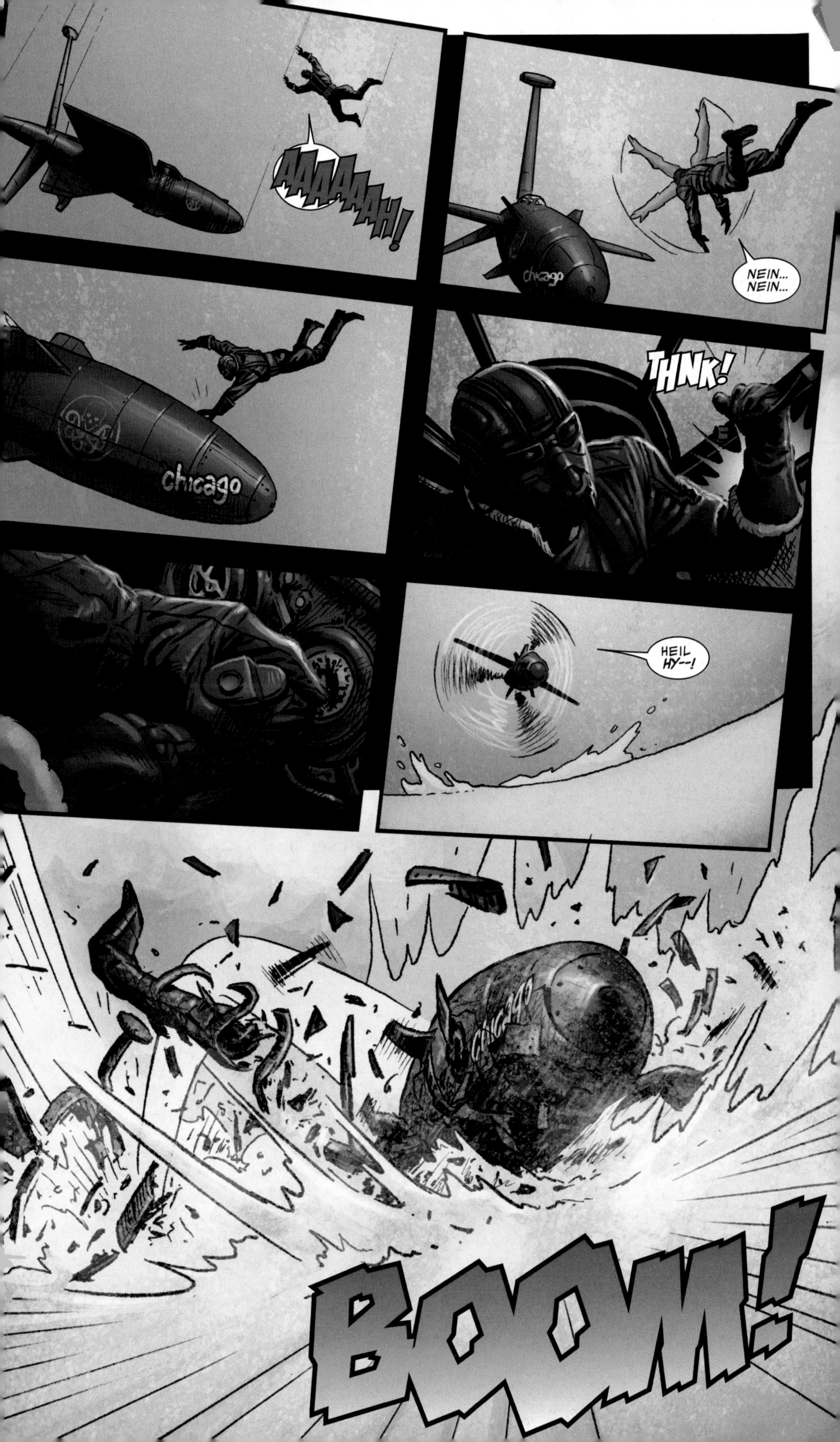
AAAAAAH!
NEIN... NEIN...
THNK!
HEIL HY--!
BOOM!

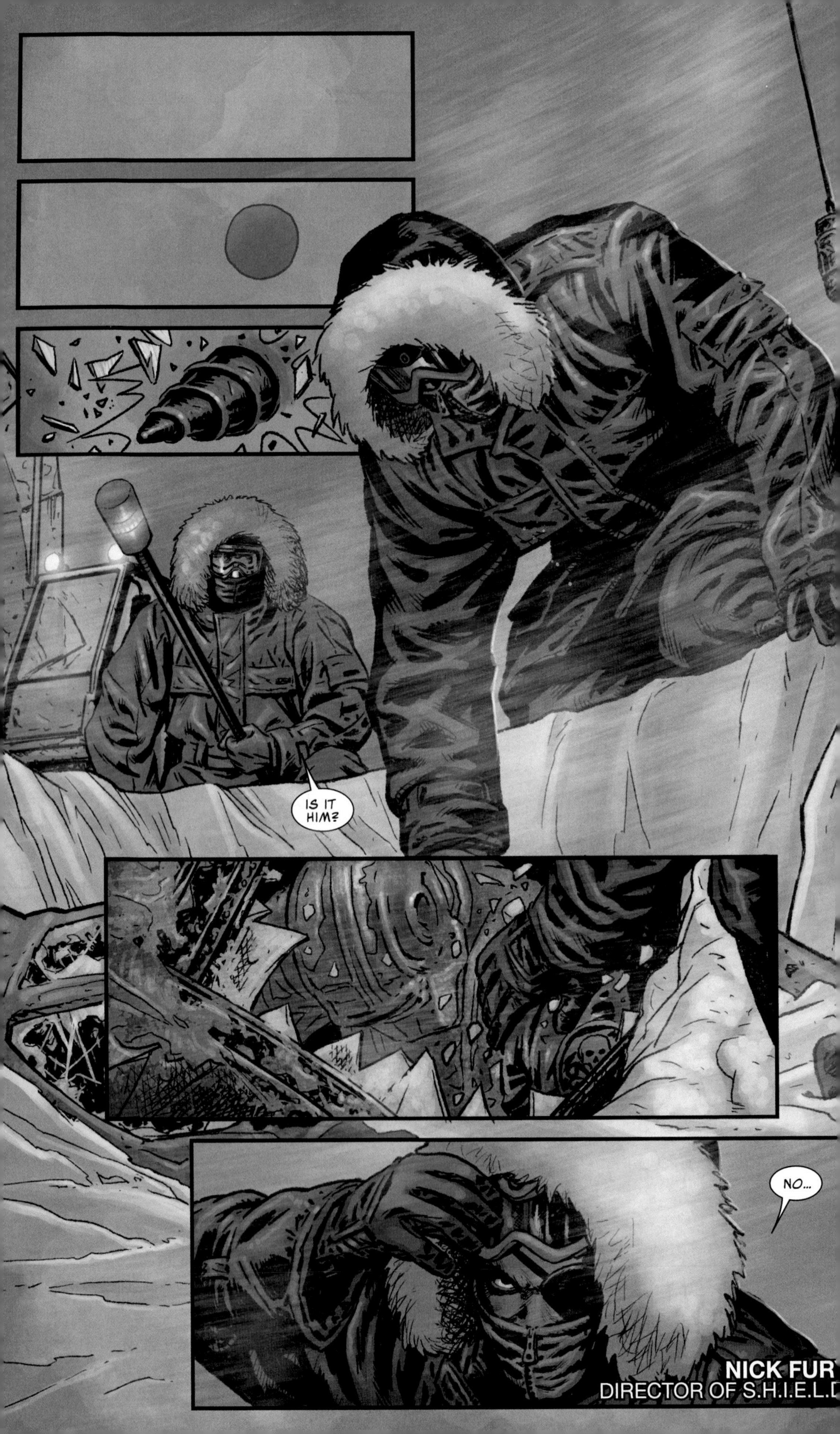
IS IT HIM?
NO...
NICK FURY
DIRECTOR OF S.H.I.E.L.D.

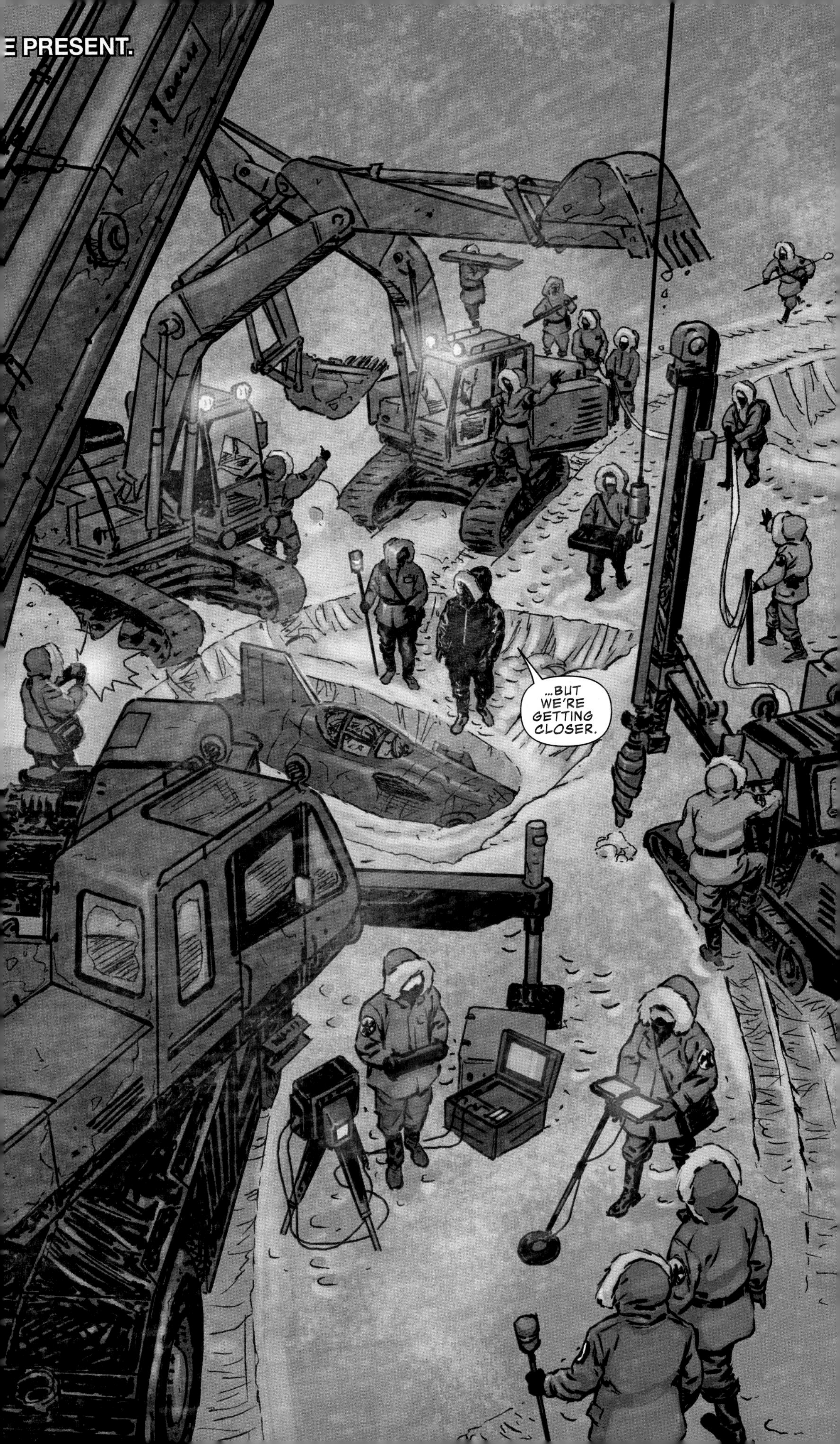
E PRESENT.
...BUT WE'RE GETTING CLOSER.

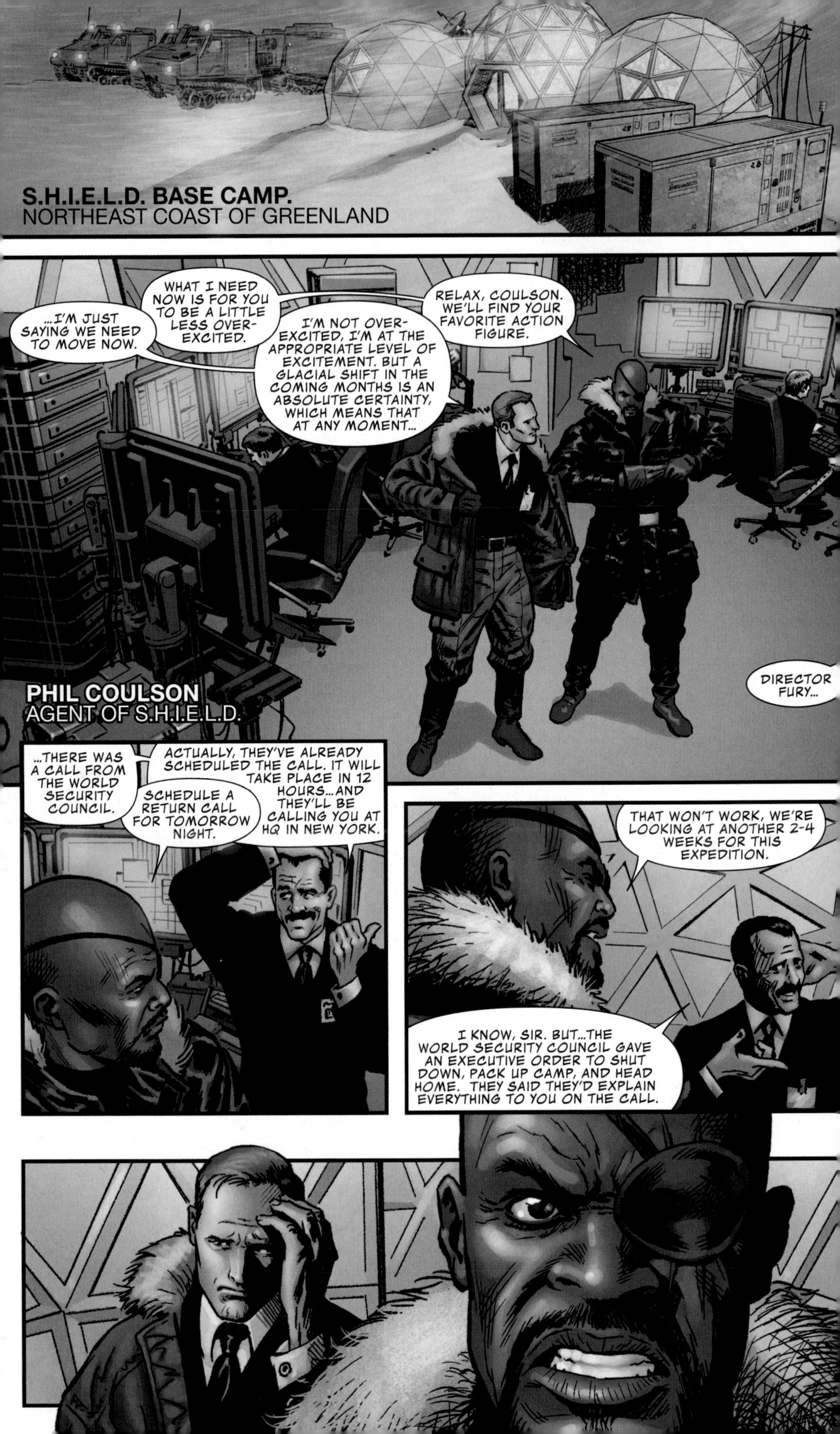

S.H.I.E.L.D. BASE CAMP.
NORTHEAST COAST OF GREENLAND
...I'M JUST SAYING WE NEED TO MOVE NOW.
WHAT I NEED NOW IS FOR YOU TO BE A LITTLE LESS OVER-EXCITED.
I'M NOT OVER-EXCITED, I'M AT THE APPROPRIATE LEVEL OF EXCITEMENT. BUT A GLACIAL SHIFT IN THE COMING MONTHS IS AN ABSOLUTE CERTAINTY, WHICH MEANS THAT AT ANY MOMENT...
RELAX, COULSON. WE'LL FIND YOUR FAVORITE ACTION FIGURE.
PHIL COULSON
AGENT OF S.H.I.E.L.D.
DIRECTOR FURY...
...THERE WAS A CALL FROM THE WORLD SECURITY COUNCIL.
SCHEDULE A RETURN CALL FOR TOMORROW NIGHT.
ACTUALLY, THEY'VE ALREADY SCHEDULED THE CALL. IT WILL TAKE PLACE IN 12 HOURS...AND THEY'LL BE CALLING YOU AT HQ IN NEW YORK.
THAT WON'T WORK, WE'RE LOOKING AT ANOTHER 2-4 WEEKS FOR THIS EXPEDITION.
I KNOW, SIR. BUT...THE WORLD SECURITY COUNCIL GAVE AN EXECUTIVE ORDER TO SHUT DOWN, PACK UP CAMP, AND HEAD HOME. THEY SAID THEY'D EXPLAIN EVERYTHING TO YOU ON THE CALL.

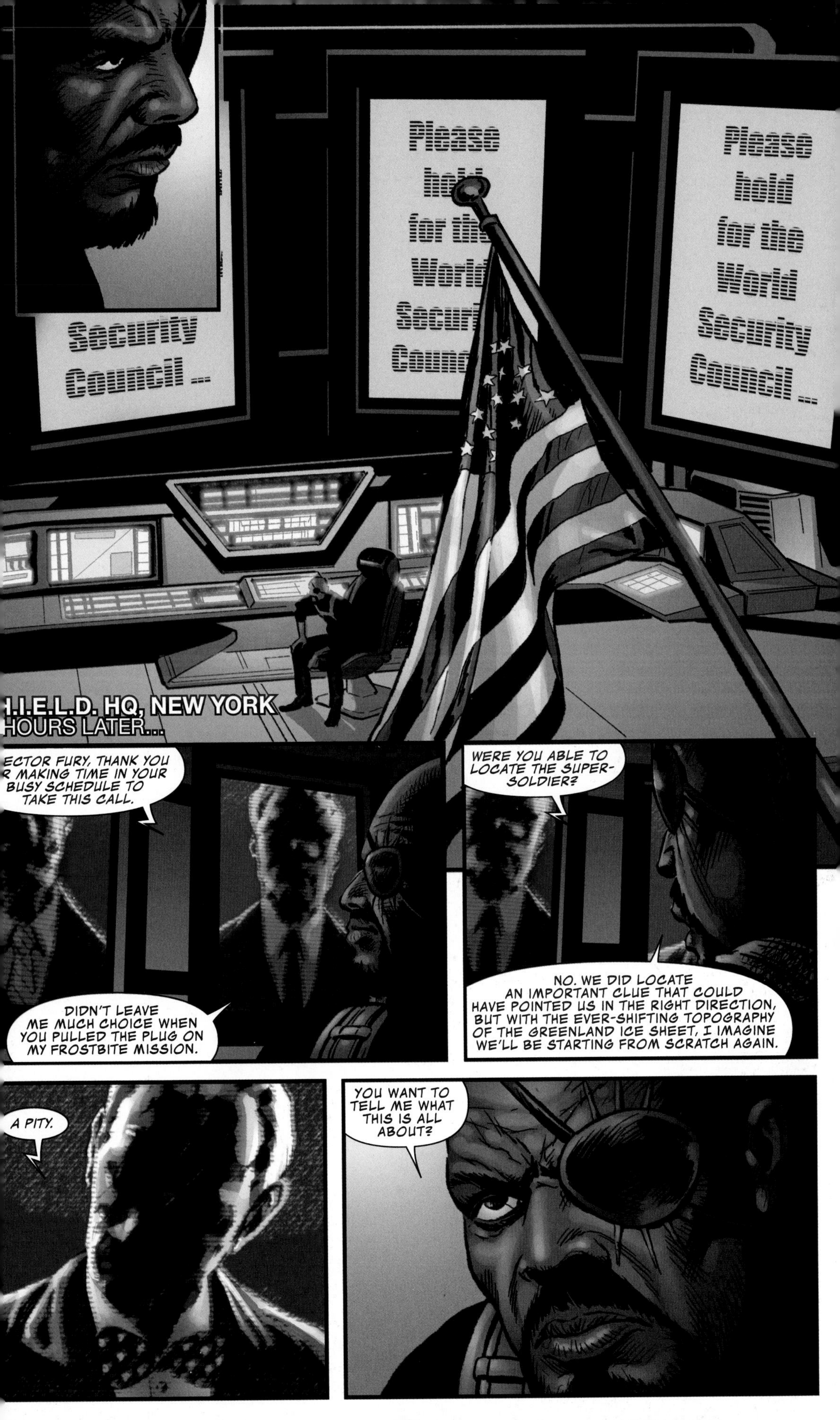
Please hold for the World Security Council ...
Security Council ...
Please hold for the World Security Council ...
.I.E.L.D. HQ, NEW YORK
HOURS LATER...
ECTOR FURY, THANK YOU
R MAKING TIME IN YOUR BUSY SCHEDULE TO TAKE THIS CALL.
DIDN'T LEAVE ME MUCH CHOICE WHEN YOU PULLED THE PLUG ON MY FROSTBITE MISSION.
WERE YOU ABLE TO LOCATE THE SUPER-SOLDIER?
NO. WE DID LOCATE AN IMPORTANT CLUE THAT COULD HAVE POINTED US IN THE RIGHT DIRECTION, BUT WITH THE EVER-SHIFTING TOPOGRAPHY OF THE GREENLAND ICE SHEET, I IMAGINE WE'LL BE STARTING FROM SCRATCH AGAIN.
A PITY.
YOU WANT TO TELL ME WHAT THIS IS ALL ABOUT?

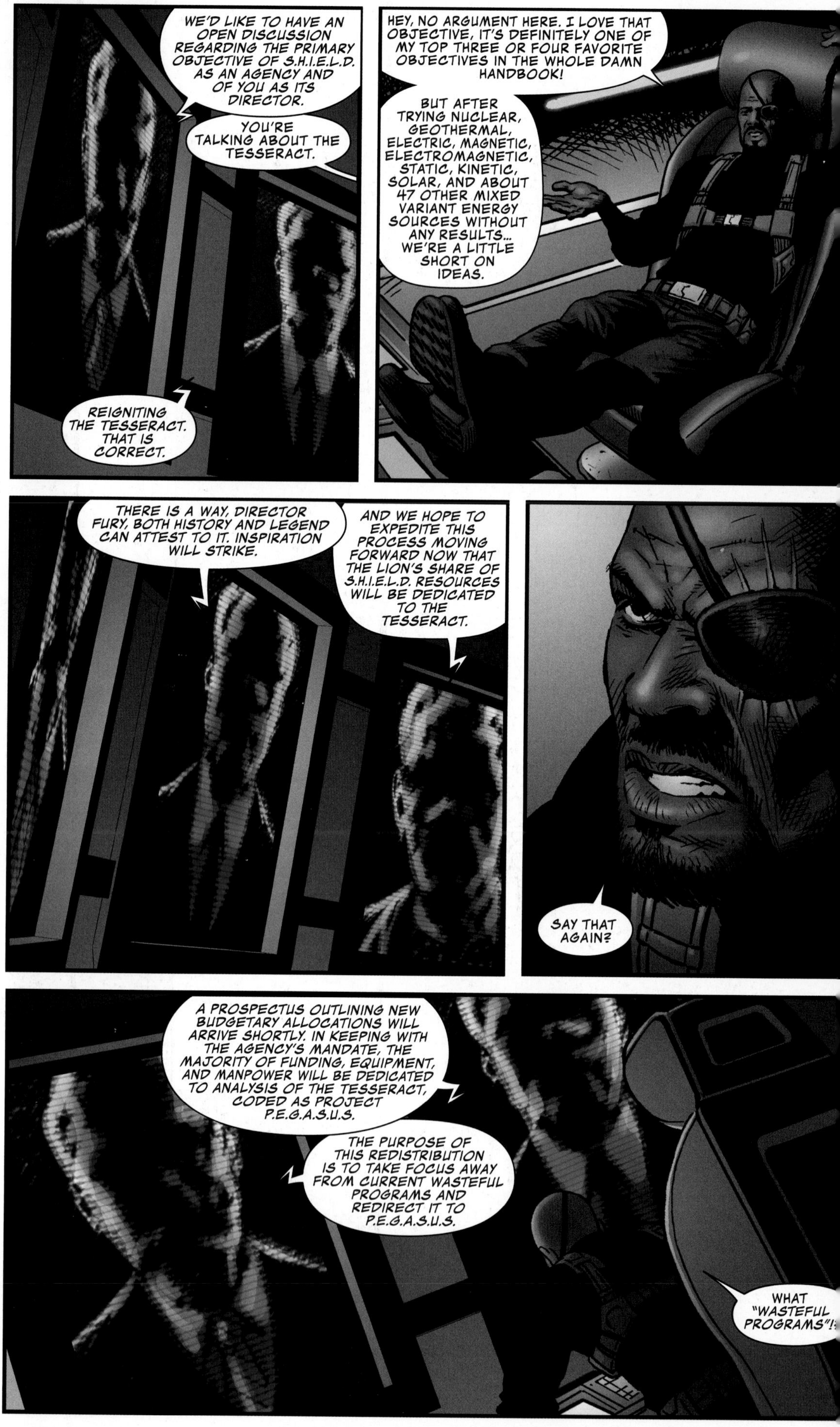
WE'D LIKE TO HAVE AN OPEN DISCUSSION REGARDING THE PRIMARY OBJECTIVE OF S.H.I.E.L.D. AS AN AGENCY AND OF YOU AS ITS DIRECTOR.
YOU'RE TALKING ABOUT THE TESSERACT.
REIGNITING THE TESSERACT. THAT IS CORRECT.
HEY, NO ARGUMENT HERE. I LOVE THAT OBJECTIVE, IT'S DEFINITELY ONE OF MY TOP THREE OR FOUR FAVORITE OBJECTIVES IN THE WHOLE DAMN HANDBOOK!
BUT AFTER TRYING NUCLEAR, GEOTHERMAL, ELECTRIC, MAGNETIC, ELECTROMAGNETIC, STATIC, KINETIC, SOLAR, AND ABOUT 47 OTHER MIXED VARIANT ENERGY SOURCES WITHOUT ANY RESULTS... WE'RE A LITTLE SHORT ON IDEAS.
THERE IS A WAY, DIRECTOR FURY, BOTH HISTORY AND LEGEND CAN ATTEST TO IT. INSPIRATION WILL STRIKE.
AND WE HOPE TO EXPEDITE THIS PROCESS MOVING FORWARD NOW THAT THE LION'S SHARE OF S.H.I.E.L.D. RESOURCES WILL BE DEDICATED TO THE TESSERACT.
SAY THAT AGAIN?
A PROSPECTUS OUTLINING NEW BUDGETARY ALLOCATIONS WILL ARRIVE SHORTLY. IN KEEPING WITH THE AGENCY'S MANDATE, THE MAJORITY OF FUNDING, EQUIPMENT, AND MANPOWER WILL BE DEDICATED TO ANALYSIS OF THE TESSERACT, CODED AS PROJECT P.E.G.A.S.U.S.
THE PURPOSE OF THIS REDISTRIBUTION IS TO TAKE FOCUS AWAY FROM CURRENT WASTEFUL PROGRAMS AND REDIRECT IT TO P.E.G.A.S.U.S.
WHAT "WASTEFUL PROGRAMS"!?

"IT IS A WASTE OF VALUABLE ASSETS TO PROLONG THE SEARCH FOR STEVE ROGERS, CONSIDERING THAT HIS PURPOSE WOULD BE INSUBSTANTIAL IN THE PRESENT DAY.

"IT IS A WASTE OF PRECIOUS TIME TO CONTINUE CODDLING TONY STARK WHEN ALL YOU NEED CONCERN YOURSELF WITH IS THE ACQUISITION OF HIS WEAPONS TECHNOLOGY.

LET THERE BE ROOOCCCK ♪♫

"IT IS A WASTE OF COUNTLESS PRODUCTIVE MAN HOURS TO MAINTAIN SURVEILLANCE ON DR. BANNER, A MAN THAT HAS LEFT YOU PERPLEXED AND UNDECIDED AS TO ANY COURSE OF ACTION REGARDING HIS EXISTENCE."

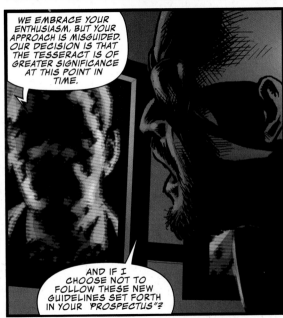

WE EMBRACE YOUR ENTHUSIASM, BUT YOUR APPROACH IS MISGUIDED. OUR DECISION IS THAT THE TESSERACT IS OF GREATER SIGNIFICANCE AT THIS POINT IN TIME.

AND IF I CHOOSE NOT TO FOLLOW THESE NEW GUIDELINES SET FORTH IN YOUR "PROSPECTUS"?

THEN YOU'LL BE REPLACED WITH SOMEONE WHO WILL.

IF IT HELPS TO PUT THIS IN PERSPECTIVE, THEN CONSIDER YOURSELF ON NOTICE, DIRECTOR FURY.

THAT TOOK A WHILE.

THEY HAD A LOT TO SAY.

ANYTHING WORTH REPEATING?

NOT IN POLITE COMPANY.

SO... WHAT DO WE DO?

WE KEEP DOING WHAT WE'RE DOING AND TELL THEM THAT WE'RE DOING WHAT THEY WANT US TO BE DOING.

HOW?

HELL, I DUNN GET CREATIV COOK THE BOO WHATEVER I TAKES TO LE US DO THIS JOB RIGHT.

...IS THAT THE BEST PLAN OF ACTION MOVING FORWARD?

IF IT'S NOT...

...WE'RE GOING TO FIND OUT THE HARD WAY.

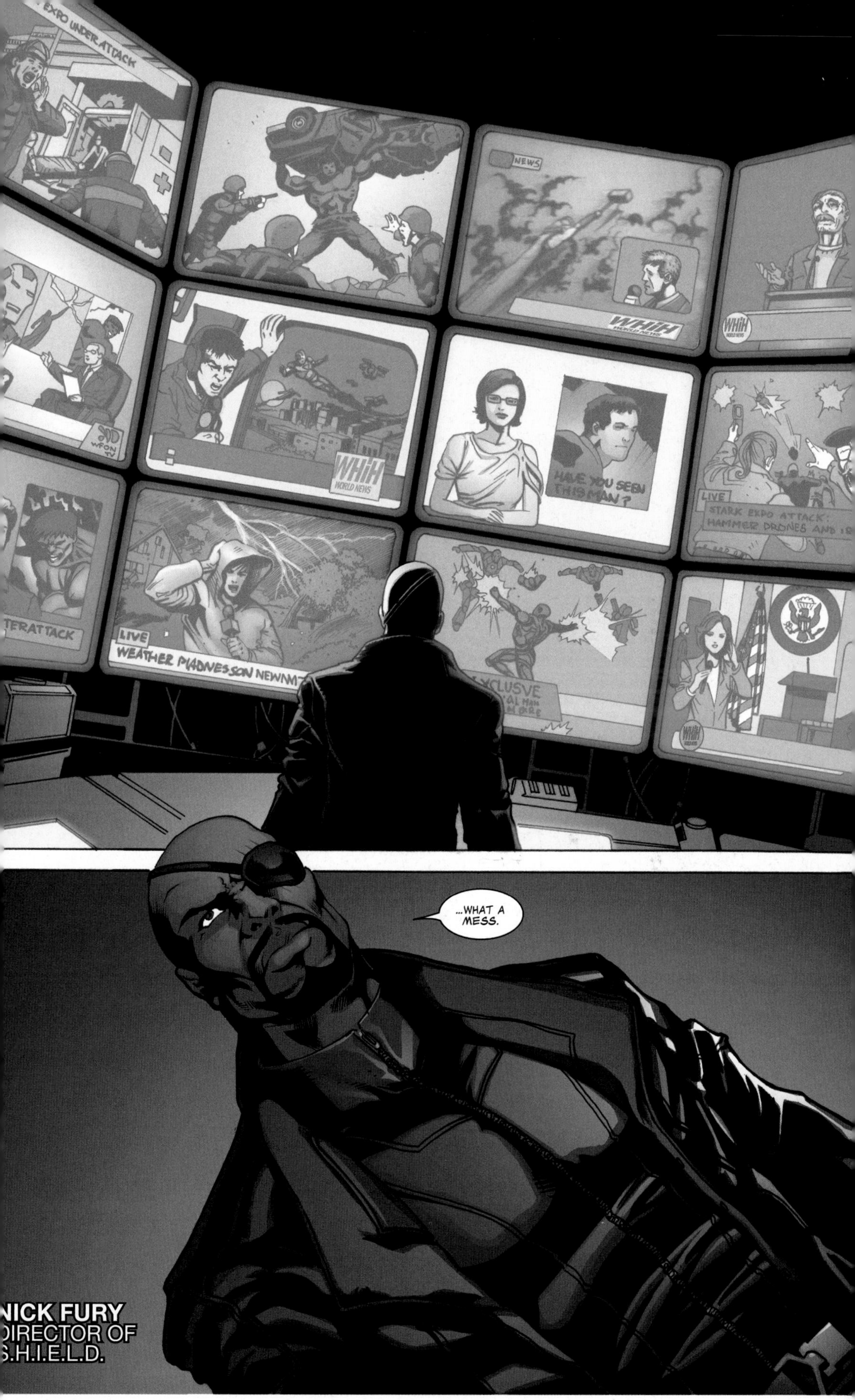
EXPO UNDER ATTACK
NEWS
WHiH WORLD NEWS
WFON TV
HAVE YOU SEEN THIS MAN?
LIVE
STARK EXPO ATTACK:
LIVE
...WHAT A MESS.
NICK FURY
DIRECTOR OF
S.H.I.E.L.D.

FURY'S B

G WEEK

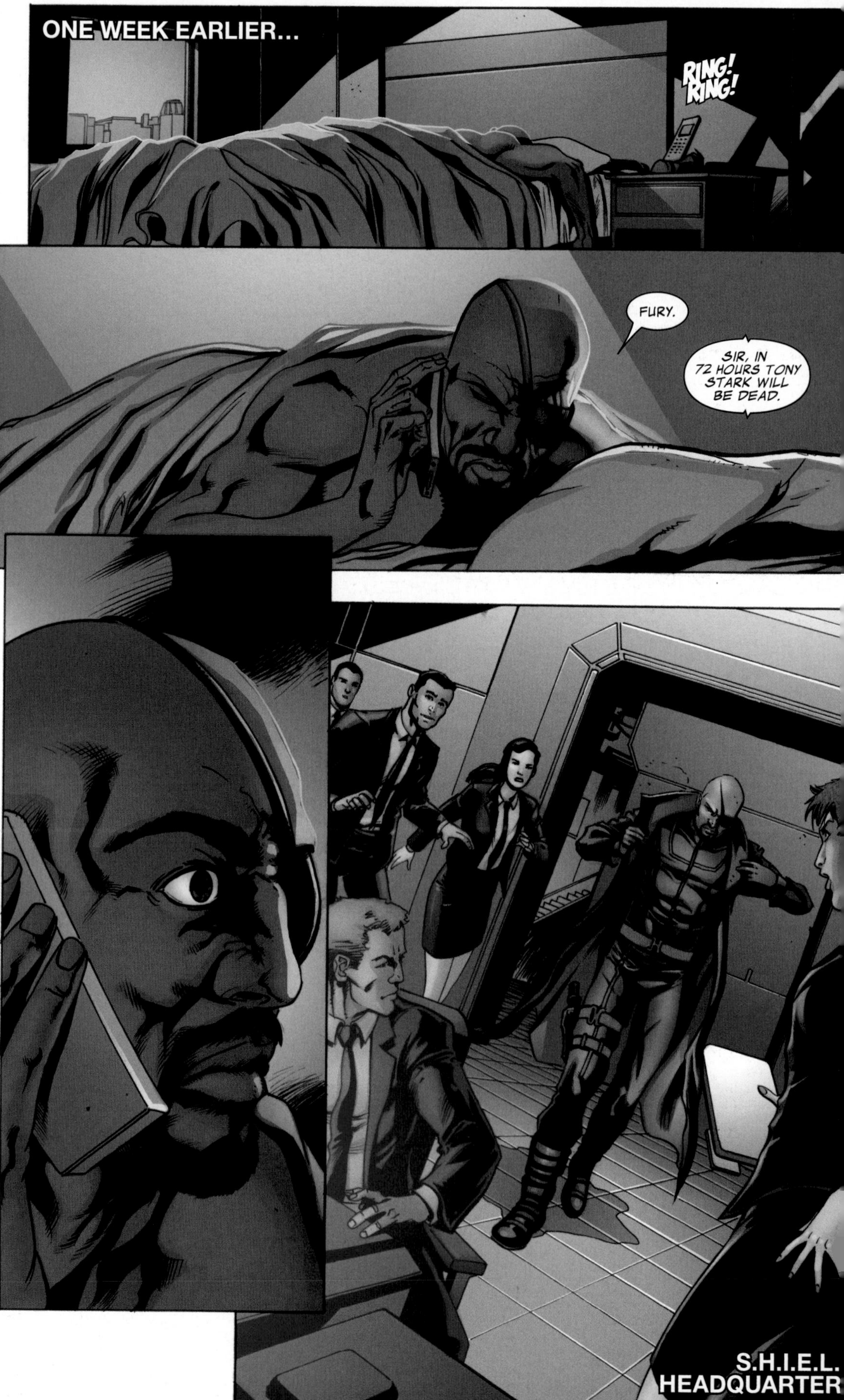
ONE WEEK EARLIER...
RING! RING!
FURY.
SIR, IN 72 HOURS TONY STARK WILL BE DEAD.
S.H.I.E.L. HEADQUARTER

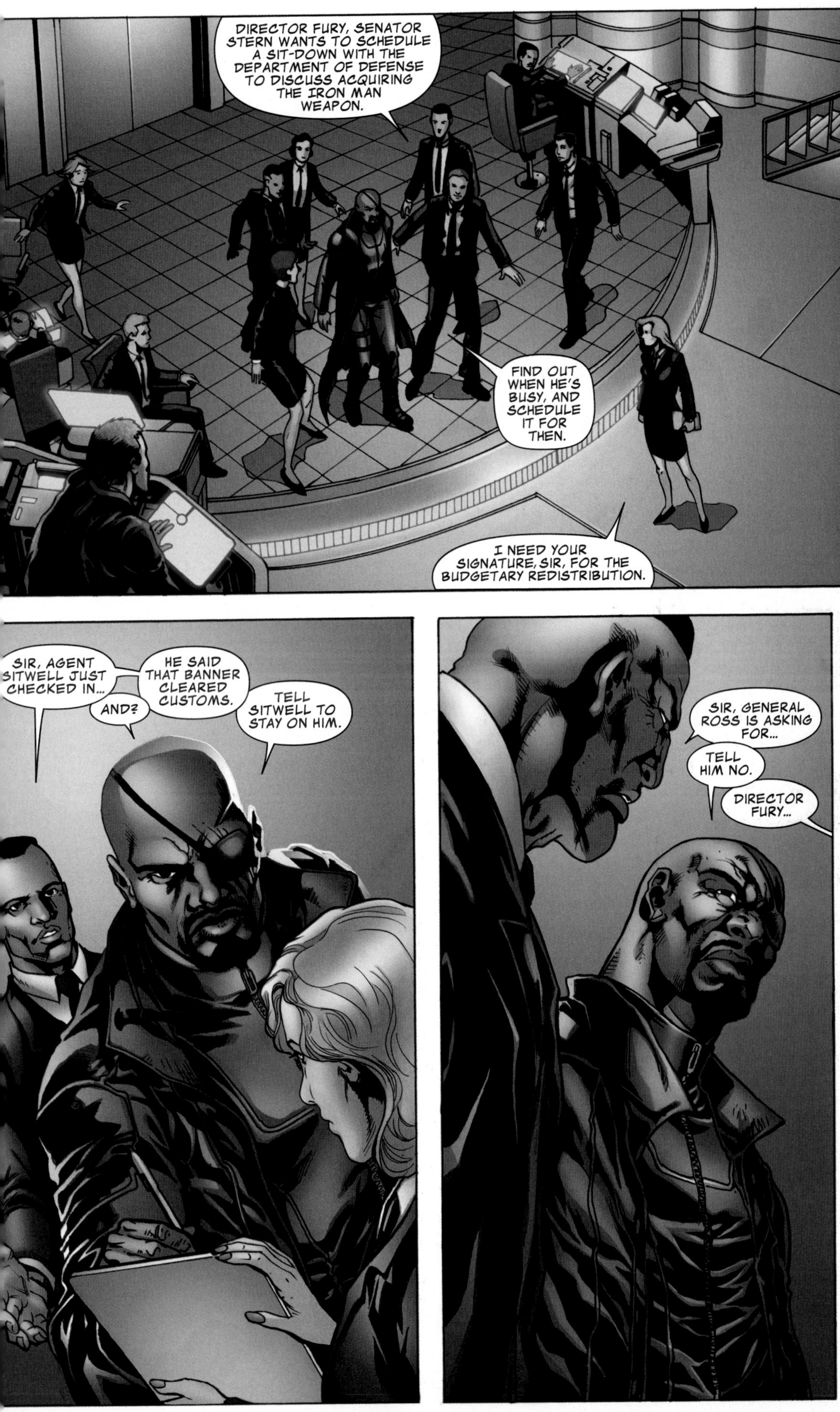
DIRECTOR FURY, SENATOR STERN WANTS TO SCHEDULE A SIT-DOWN WITH THE DEPARTMENT OF DEFENSE TO DISCUSS ACQUIRING THE IRON MAN WEAPON.
FIND OUT WHEN HE'S BUSY, AND SCHEDULE IT FOR THEN.
I NEED YOUR SIGNATURE, SIR, FOR THE BUDGETARY REDISTRIBUTION.
SIR, AGENT SITWELL JUST CHECKED IN...
AND?
HE SAID THAT BANNER CLEARED CUSTOMS.
TELL SITWELL TO STAY ON HIM.
SIR, GENERAL ROSS IS ASKING FOR...
TELL HIM NO.
DIRECTOR FURY...

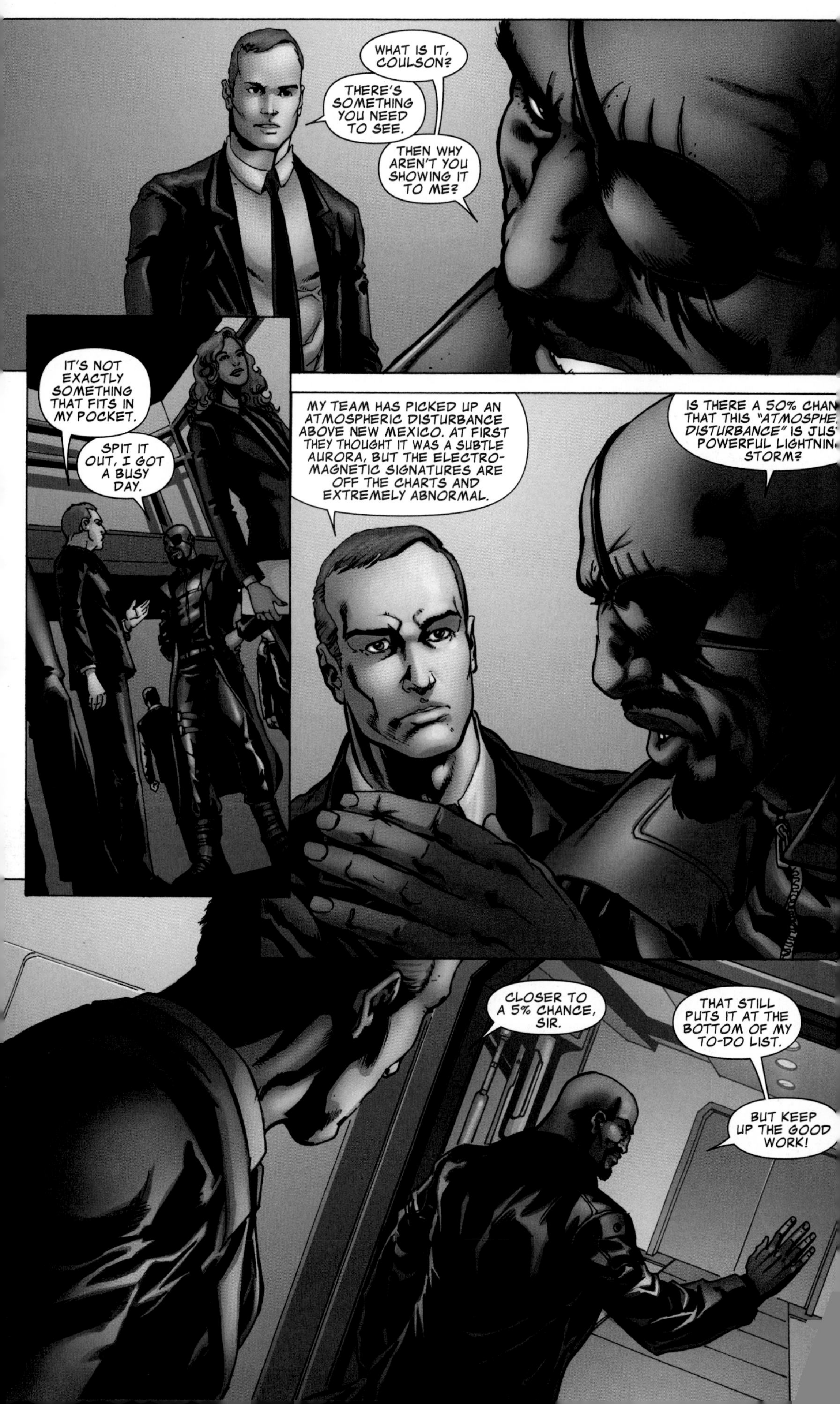

WHAT IS IT, COULSON?
THERE'S SOMETHING YOU NEED TO SEE.
THEN WHY AREN'T YOU SHOWING IT TO ME?
IT'S NOT EXACTLY SOMETHING THAT FITS IN MY POCKET.
SPIT IT OUT, I GOT A BUSY DAY.
MY TEAM HAS PICKED UP AN ATMOSPHERIC DISTURBANCE ABOVE NEW MEXICO. AT FIRST THEY THOUGHT IT WAS A SUBTLE AURORA, BUT THE ELECTRO-MAGNETIC SIGNATURES ARE OFF THE CHARTS AND EXTREMELY ABNORMAL.
IS THERE A 50% CHAN THAT THIS "ATMOSPHE DISTURBANCE" IS JUS POWERFUL LIGHTNIN STORM?
CLOSER TO A 5% CHANCE, SIR.
THAT STILL PUTS IT AT THE BOTTOM OF MY TO-DO LIST.
BUT KEEP UP THE GOOD WORK!

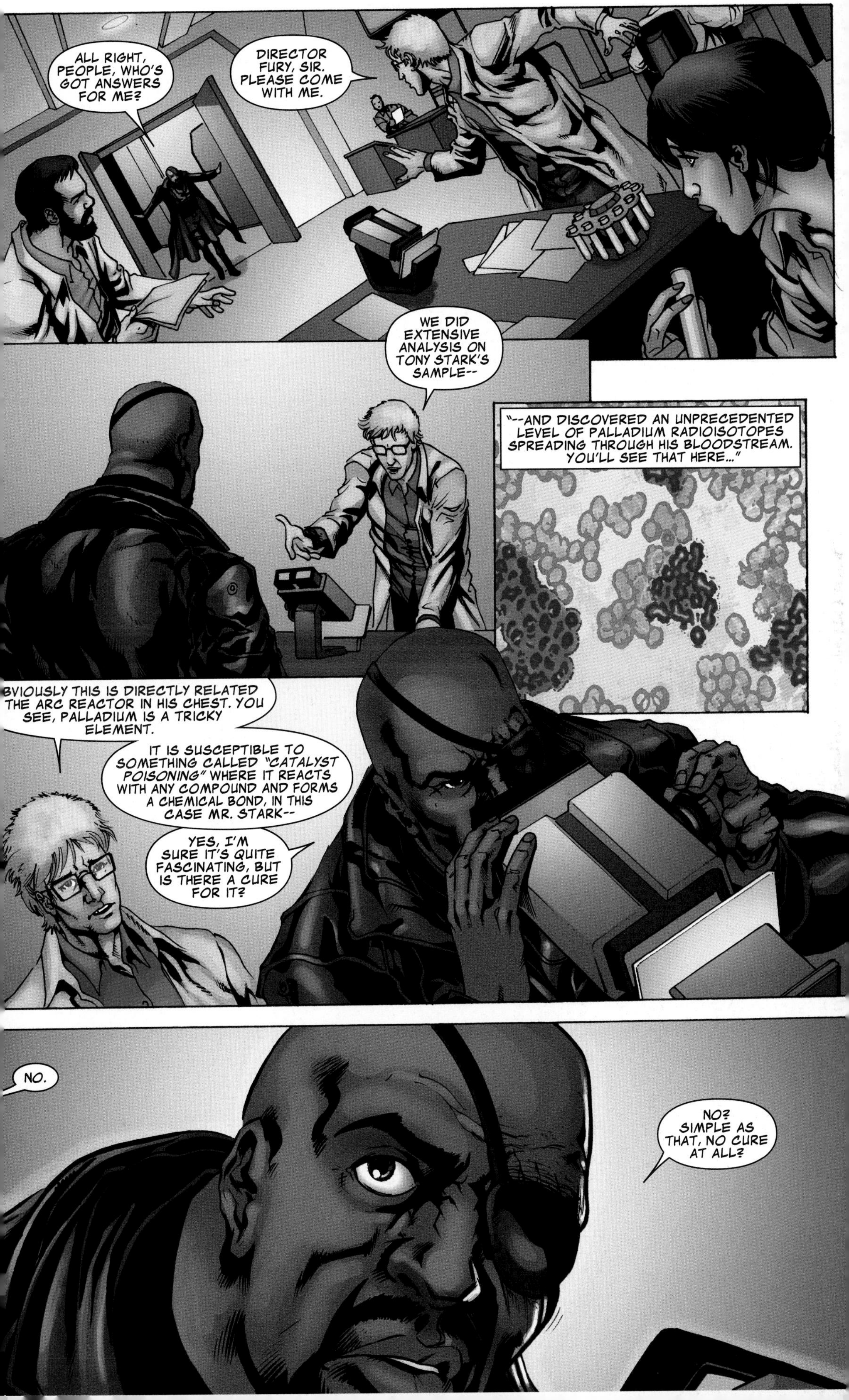
ALL RIGHT, PEOPLE, WHO'S GOT ANSWERS FOR ME?
DIRECTOR FURY, SIR. PLEASE COME WITH ME.
WE DID EXTENSIVE ANALYSIS ON TONY STARK'S SAMPLE--
"--AND DISCOVERED AN UNPRECEDENTED LEVEL OF PALLADIUM RADIOISOTOPES SPREADING THROUGH HIS BLOODSTREAM. YOU'LL SEE THAT HERE..."
BVIOUSLY THIS IS DIRECTLY RELATED THE ARC REACTOR IN HIS CHEST. YOU SEE, PALLADIUM IS A TRICKY ELEMENT.
IT IS SUSCEPTIBLE TO SOMETHING CALLED "CATALYST POISONING" WHERE IT REACTS WITH ANY COMPOUND AND FORMS A CHEMICAL BOND, IN THIS CASE MR. STARK--
YES, I'M SURE IT'S QUITE FASCINATING, BUT IS THERE A CURE FOR IT?
NO.
NO? SIMPLE AS THAT, NO CURE AT ALL?

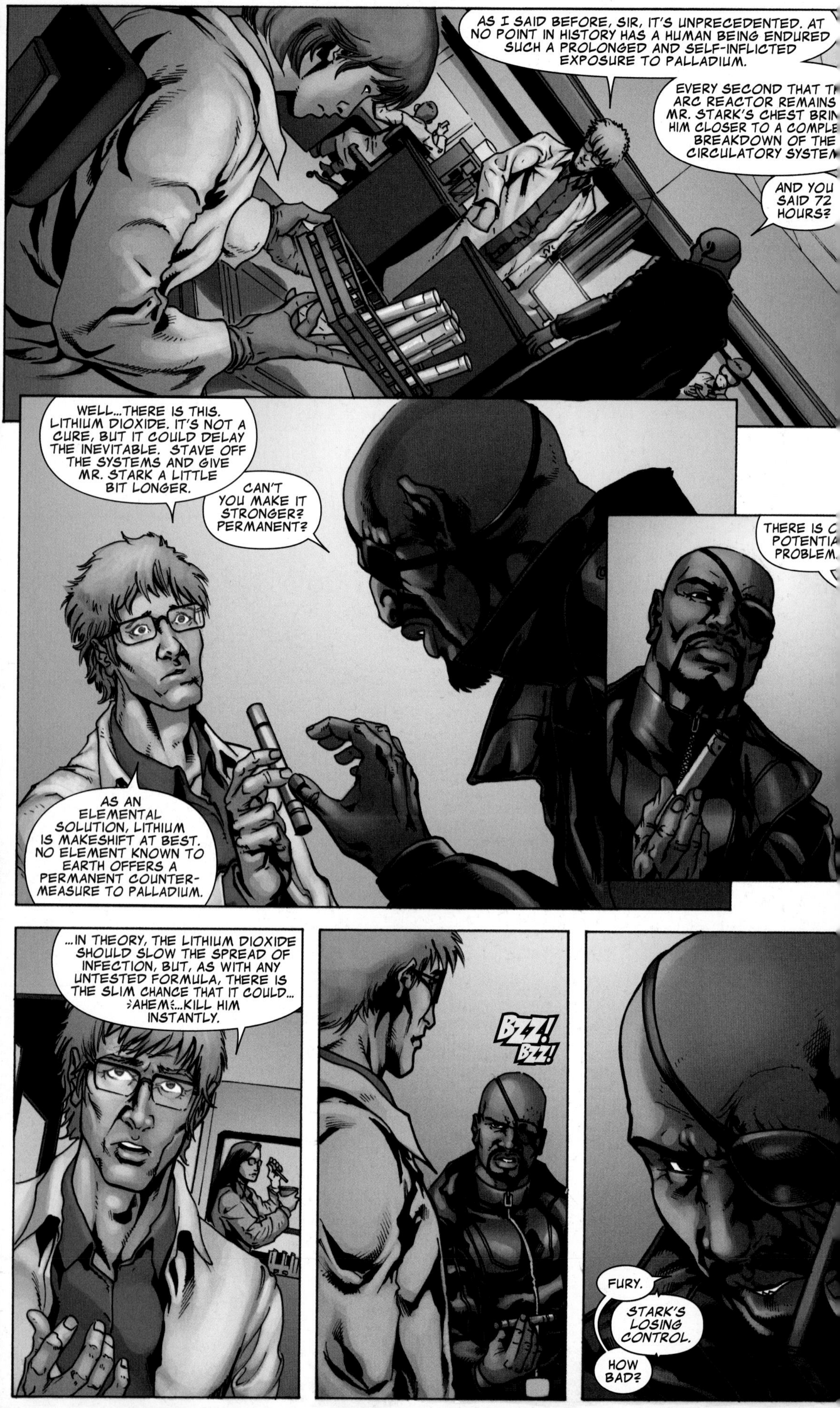
AS I SAID BEFORE, SIR, IT'S UNPRECEDENTED. AT NO POINT IN HISTORY HAS A HUMAN BEING ENDURED SUCH A PROLONGED AND SELF-INFLICTED EXPOSURE TO PALLADIUM.
EVERY SECOND THAT TH ARC REACTOR REMAINS MR. STARK'S CHEST BRIN HIM CLOSER TO A COMPLE BREAKDOWN OF THE CIRCULATORY SYSTEM
AND YOU SAID 72 HOURS?
WELL...THERE IS THIS. LITHIUM DIOXIDE. IT'S NOT A CURE, BUT IT COULD DELAY THE INEVITABLE. STAVE OFF THE SYSTEMS AND GIVE MR. STARK A LITTLE BIT LONGER.
CAN'T YOU MAKE IT STRONGER? PERMANENT?
AS AN ELEMENTAL SOLUTION, LITHIUM IS MAKESHIFT AT BEST. NO ELEMENT KNOWN TO EARTH OFFERS A PERMANENT COUNTER-MEASURE TO PALLADIUM.
THERE IS C POTENTIA PROBLEM.
...IN THEORY, THE LITHIUM DIOXIDE SHOULD SLOW THE SPREAD OF INFECTION, BUT, AS WITH ANY UNTESTED FORMULA, THERE IS THE SLIM CHANCE THAT IT COULD... AHEM...KILL HIM INSTANTLY.
BZZ! BZZ!
FURY.
STARK'S LOSING CONTROL.
HOW BAD?

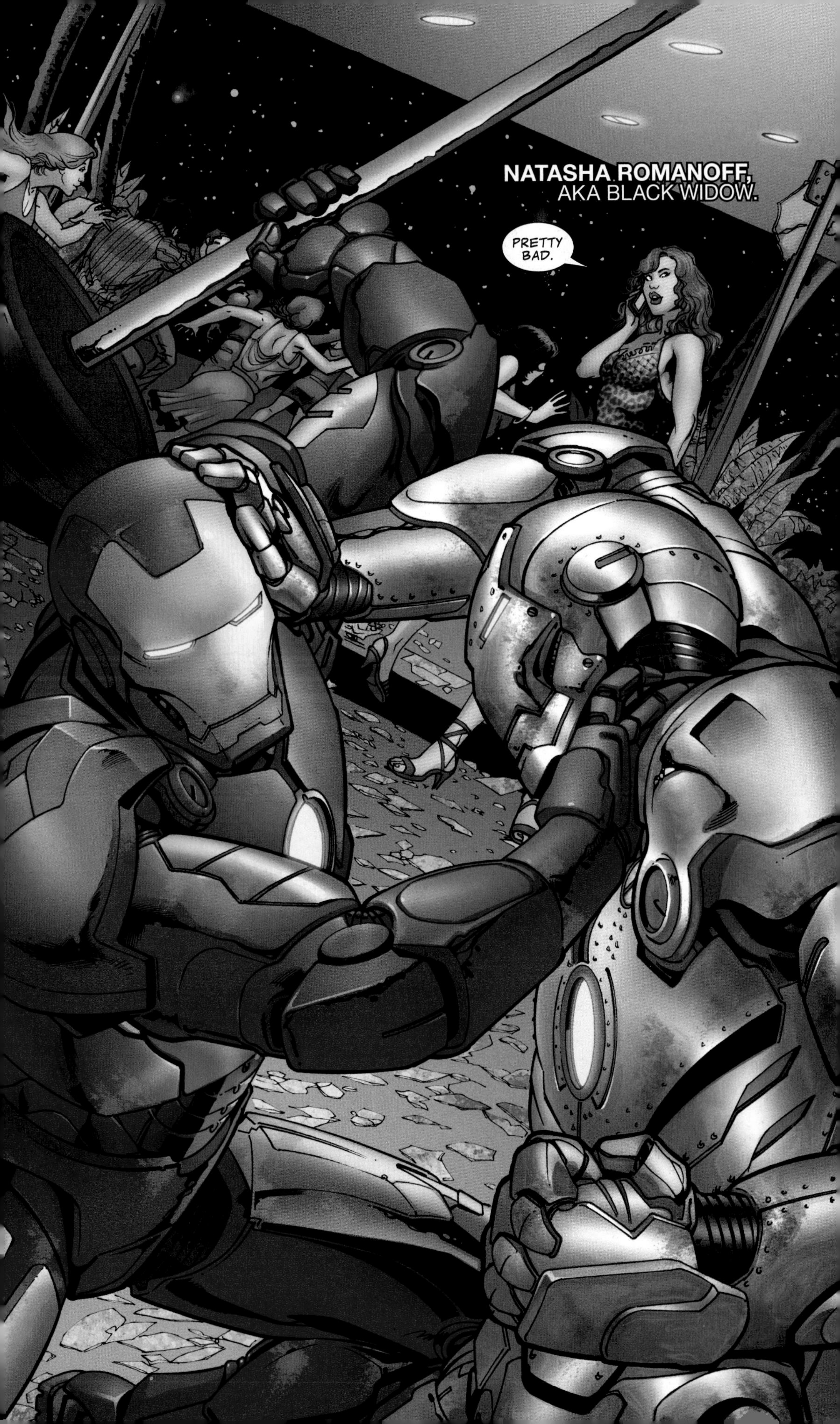
NATASHA ROMANOFF, AKA BLACK WIDOW.
PRETTY BAD.

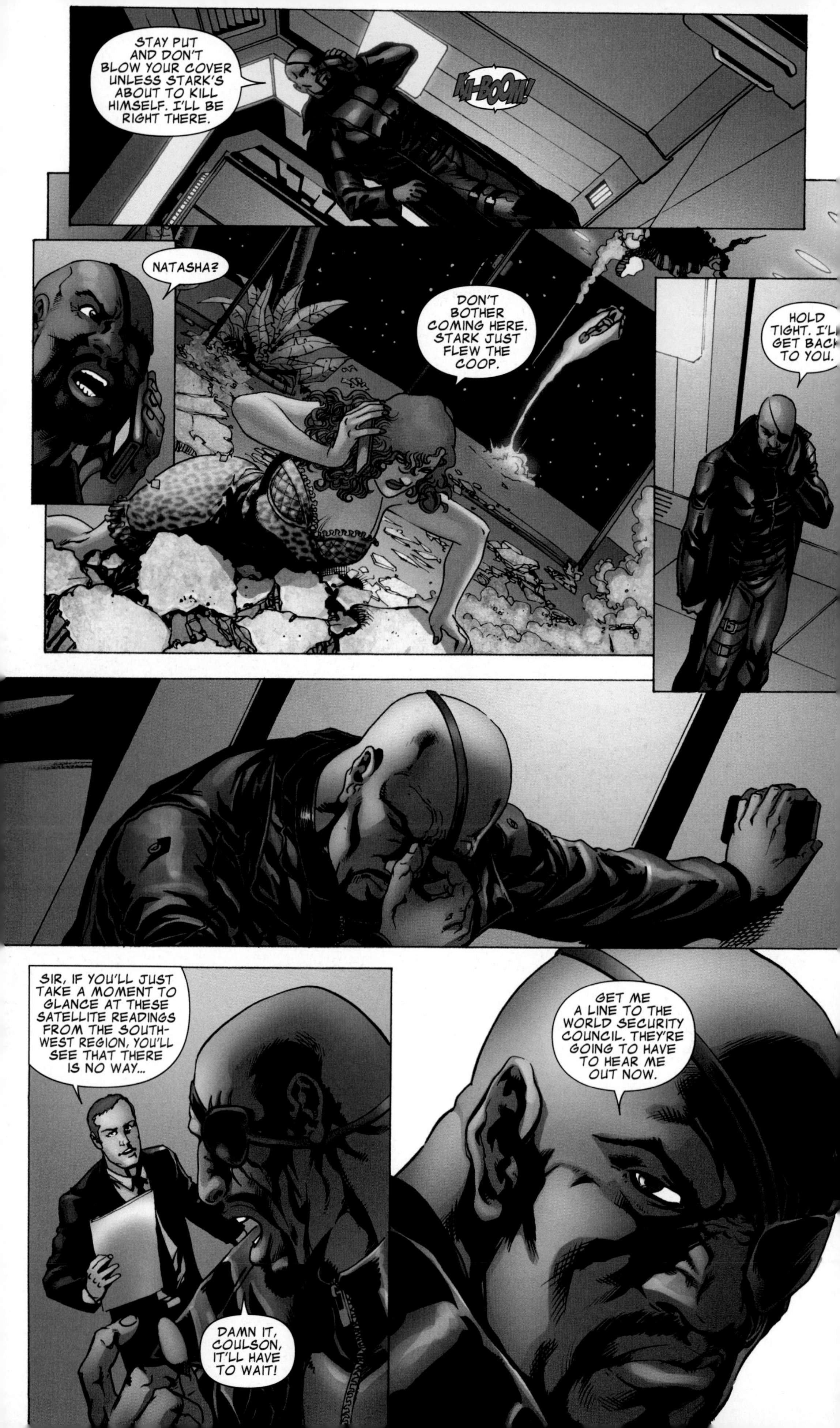
STAY PUT AND DON'T BLOW YOUR COVER UNLESS STARK'S ABOUT TO KILL HIMSELF. I'LL BE RIGHT THERE.
KA-BOOM!
NATASHA?
DON'T BOTHER COMING HERE. STARK JUST FLEW THE COOP.
HOLD TIGHT. I'LL GET BACK TO YOU.
SIR, IF YOU'LL JUST TAKE A MOMENT TO GLANCE AT THESE SATELLITE READINGS FROM THE SOUTH-WEST REGION, YOU'LL SEE THAT THERE IS NO WAY...
DAMN IT, COULSON, IT'LL HAVE TO WAIT!
GET ME A LINE TO THE WORLD SECURITY COUNCIL. THEY'RE GOING TO HAVE TO HEAR ME OUT NOW.

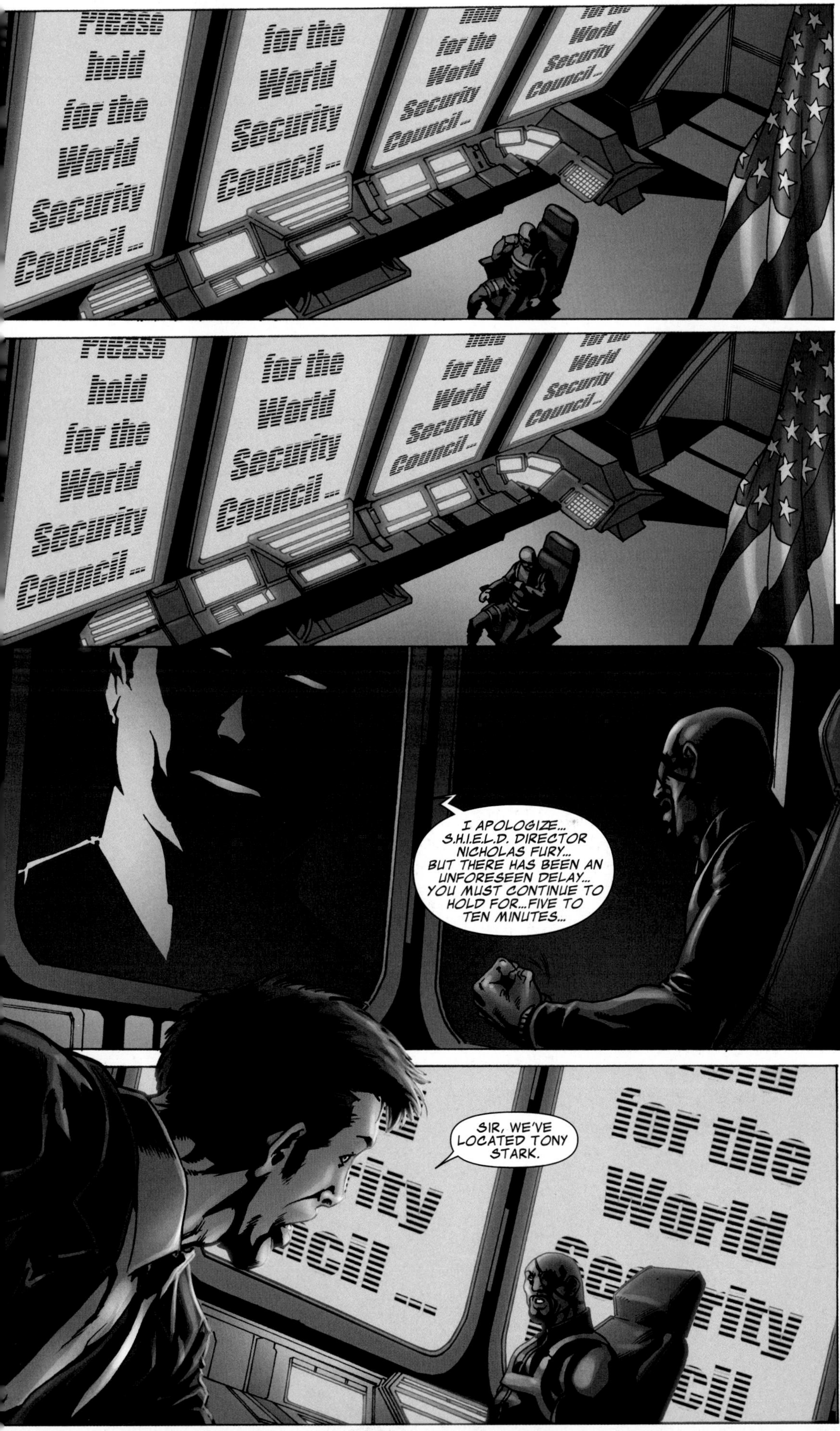
Please hold for the World Security Council...
for the World Security Council...
hold for the World Security Council...
for the World Security Council...
Please hold for the World Security Council...
for the World Security Council...
hold for the World Security Council...
for the World Security Council...
I APOLOGIZE... S.H.I.E.L.D. DIRECTOR NICHOLAS FURY... BUT THERE HAS BEEN AN UNFORESEEN DELAY... YOU MUST CONTINUE TO HOLD FOR...FIVE TO TEN MINUTES...
SIR, WE'VE LOCATED TONY STARK.
for the World

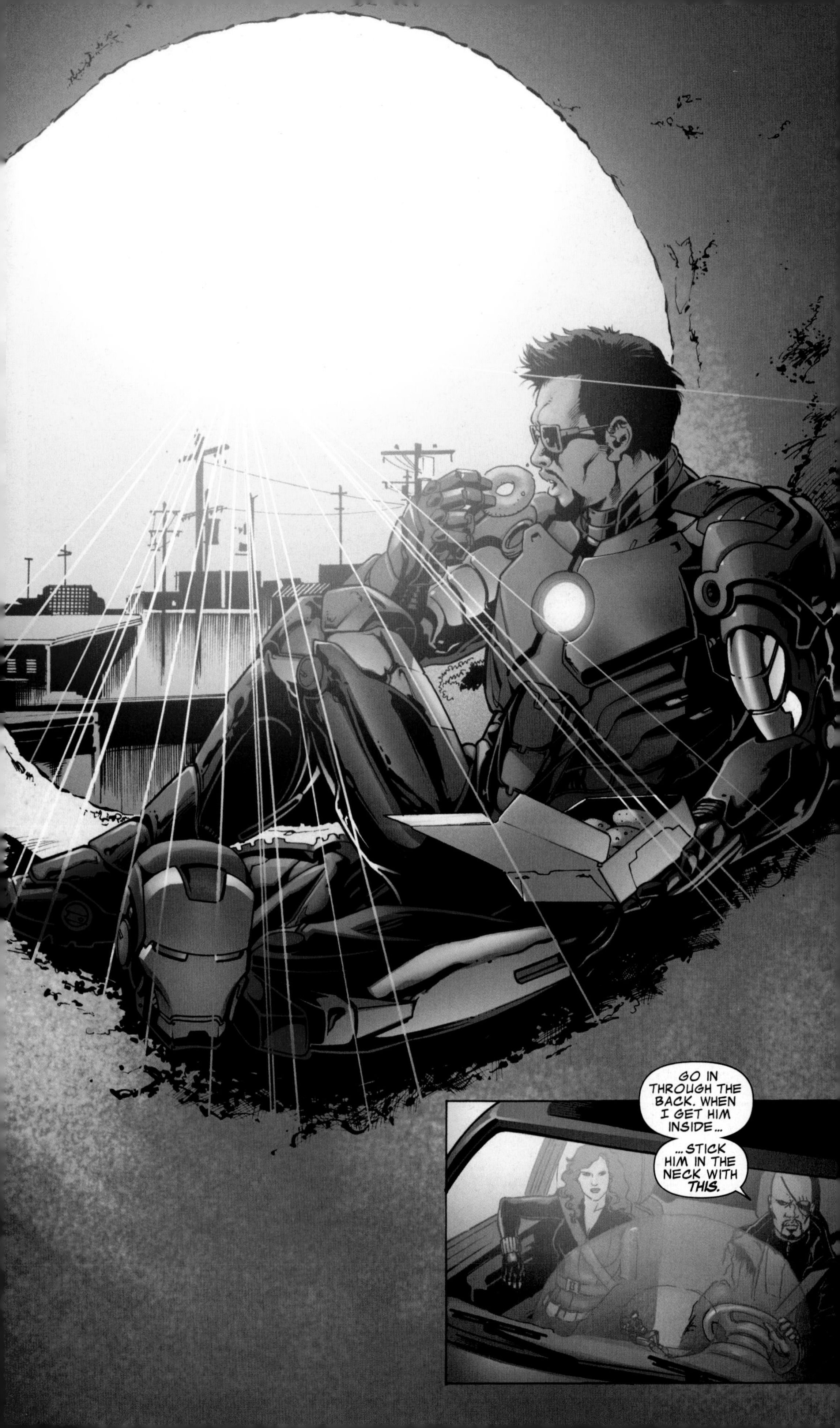
GO IN THROUGH THE BACK. WHEN I GET HIM INSIDE...
...STICK HIM IN THE NECK WITH THIS.

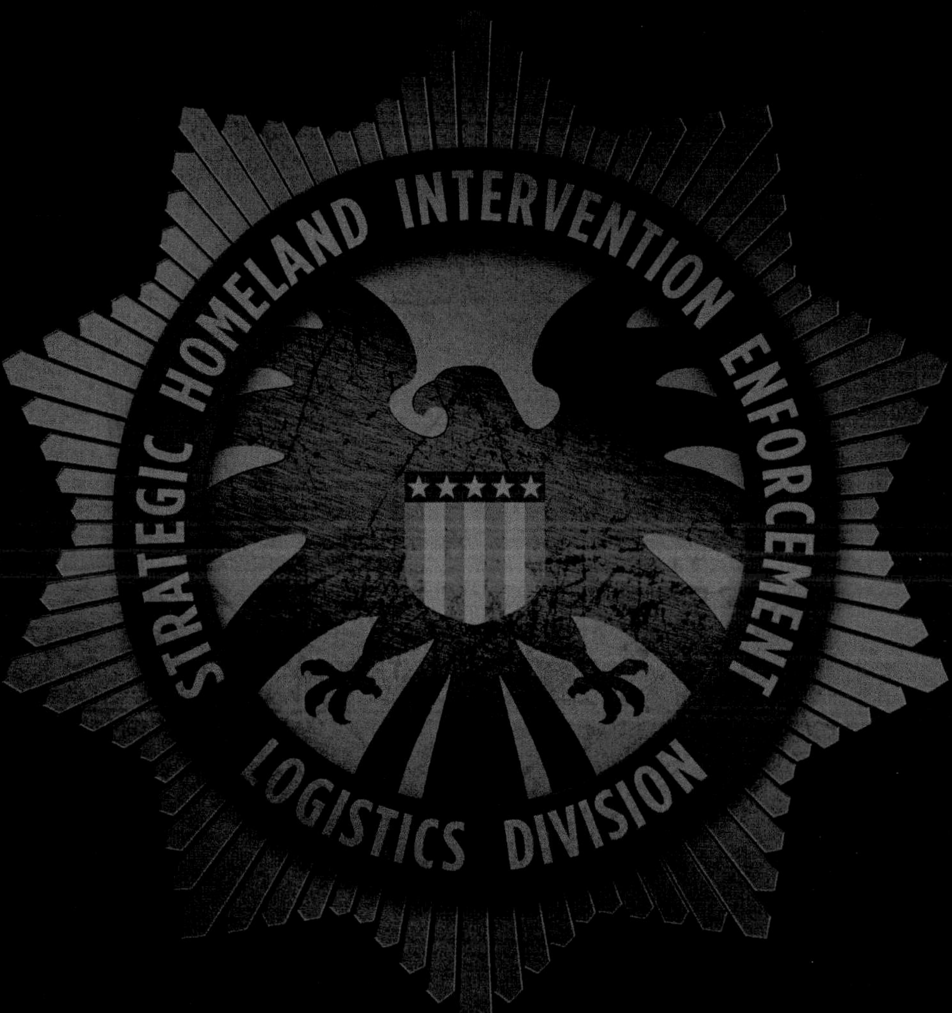
STRATEGIC HOMELAND INTERVENTION ENFORCEMENT
LOGISTICS DIVISION

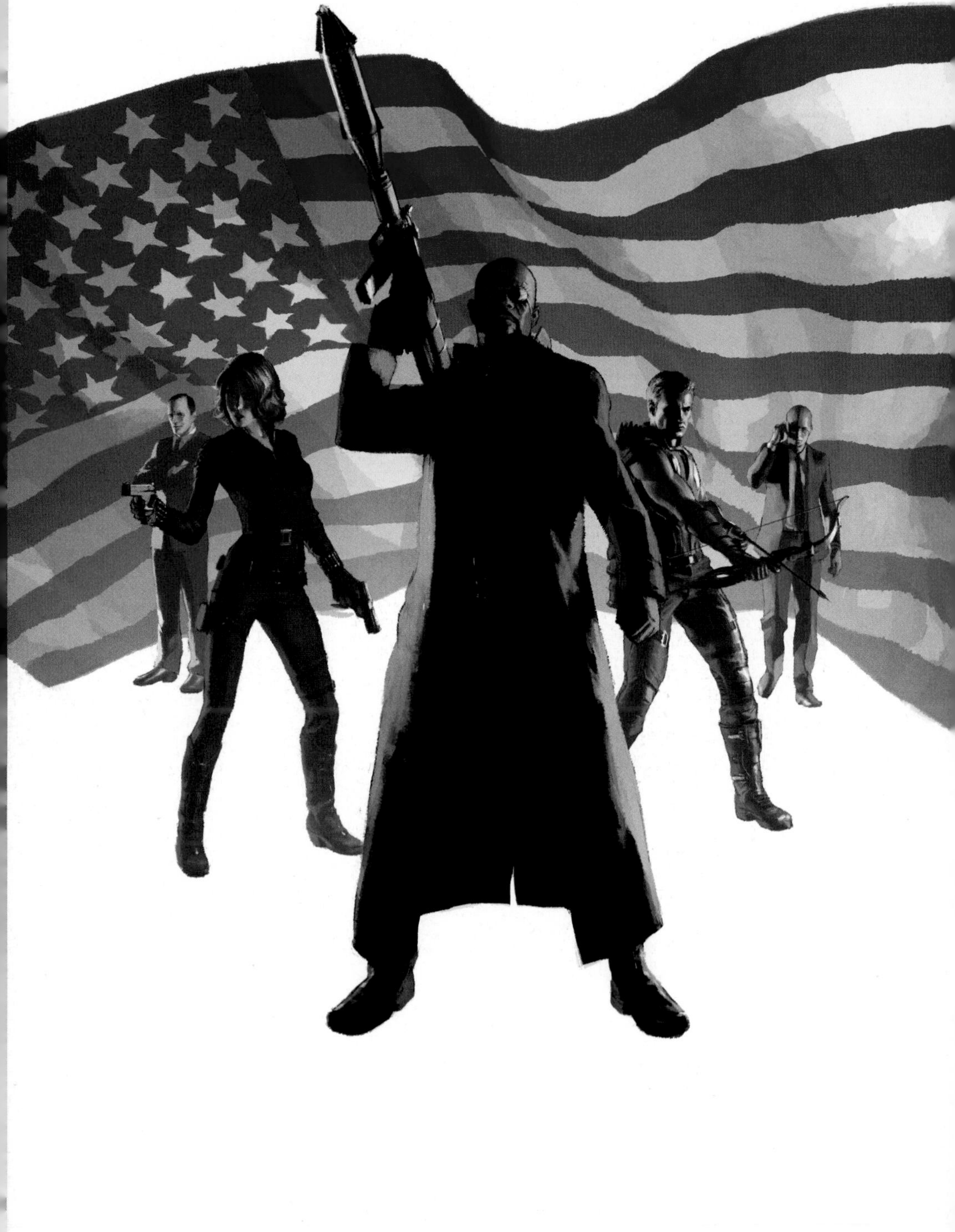

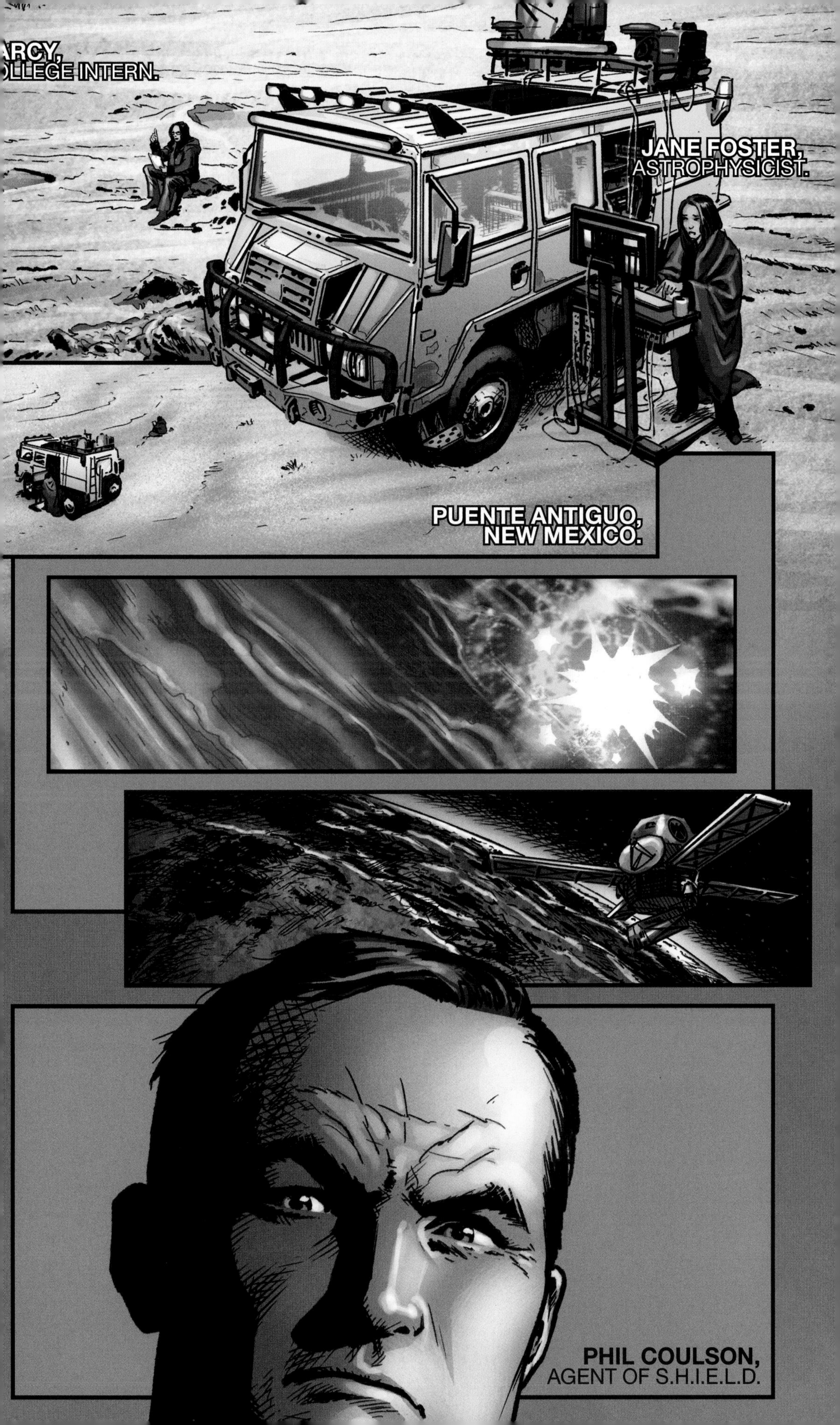

ARCY,
OLLEGE INTERN.
JANE FOSTER,
ASTROPHYSICIST.
PUENTE ANTIGUO,
NEW MEXICO.
PHIL COULSON,
AGENT OF S.H.I.E.L.D.

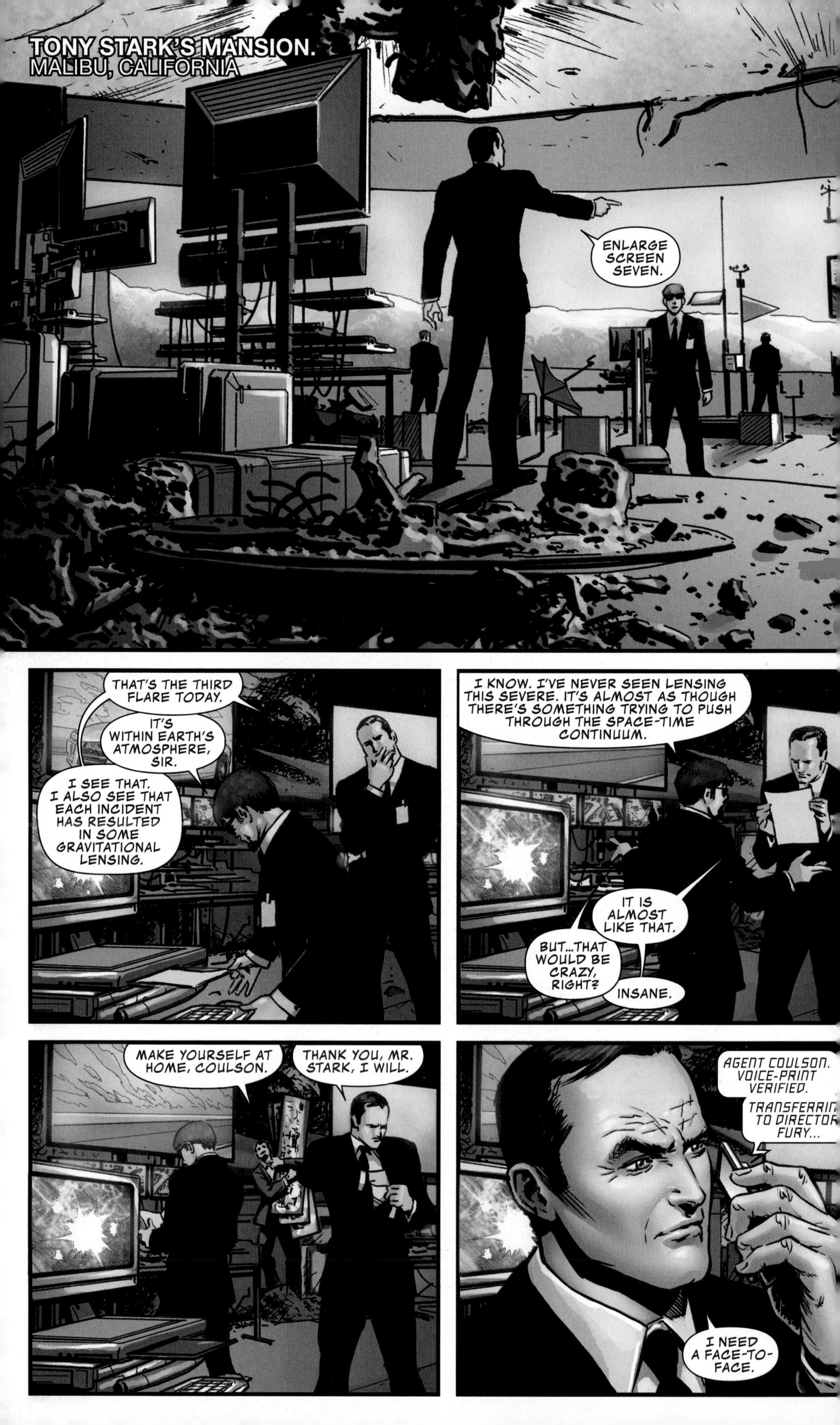
TONY STARK'S MANSION.
MALIBU, CALIFORNIA
ENLARGE SCREEN SEVEN.
THAT'S THE THIRD FLARE TODAY.
IT'S WITHIN EARTH'S ATMOSPHERE, SIR.
I SEE THAT. I ALSO SEE THAT EACH INCIDENT HAS RESULTED IN SOME GRAVITATIONAL LENSING.
I KNOW. I'VE NEVER SEEN LENSING THIS SEVERE. IT'S ALMOST AS THOUGH THERE'S SOMETHING TRYING TO PUSH THROUGH THE SPACE-TIME CONTINUUM.
IT IS ALMOST LIKE THAT.
BUT...THAT WOULD BE CRAZY, RIGHT?
INSANE.
MAKE YOURSELF AT HOME, COULSON.
THANK YOU, MR. STARK, I WILL.
AGENT COULSON. VOICE-PRINT VERIFIED.
TRANSFERRIN TO DIRECTOR FURY...
I NEED A FACE-TO-FACE.

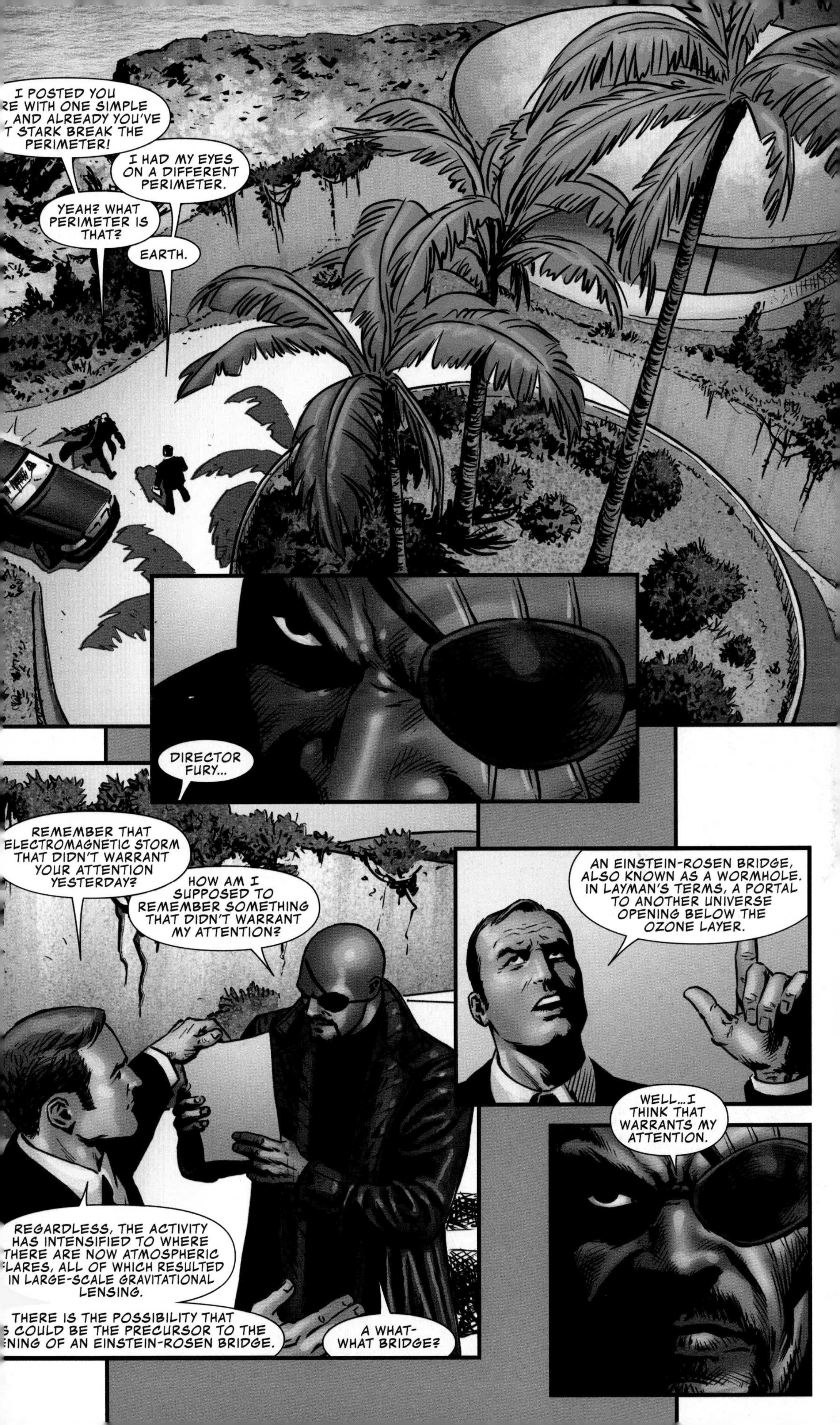
I POSTED YOU
RE WITH ONE SIMPLE
, AND ALREADY YOU'VE
T STARK BREAK THE
PERIMETER!
I HAD MY EYES
ON A DIFFERENT
PERIMETER.
YEAH? WHAT
PERIMETER IS
THAT?
EARTH.
DIRECTOR
FURY...
REMEMBER THAT
ELECTROMAGNETIC STORM
THAT DIDN'T WARRANT
YOUR ATTENTION
YESTERDAY?
HOW AM I
SUPPOSED TO
REMEMBER SOMETHING
THAT DIDN'T WARRANT
MY ATTENTION?
REGARDLESS, THE ACTIVITY
HAS INTENSIFIED TO WHERE
THERE ARE NOW ATMOSPHERIC
FLARES, ALL OF WHICH RESULTED
IN LARGE-SCALE GRAVITATIONAL
LENSING.
THERE IS THE POSSIBILITY THAT
S COULD BE THE PRECURSOR TO THE
ENING OF AN EINSTEIN-ROSEN BRIDGE.
A WHAT-
WHAT BRIDGE?
AN EINSTEIN-ROSEN BRIDGE,
ALSO KNOWN AS A WORMHOLE.
IN LAYMAN'S TERMS, A PORTAL
TO ANOTHER UNIVERSE
OPENING BELOW THE
OZONE LAYER.
WELL...I
THINK THAT
WARRANTS MY
ATTENTION.

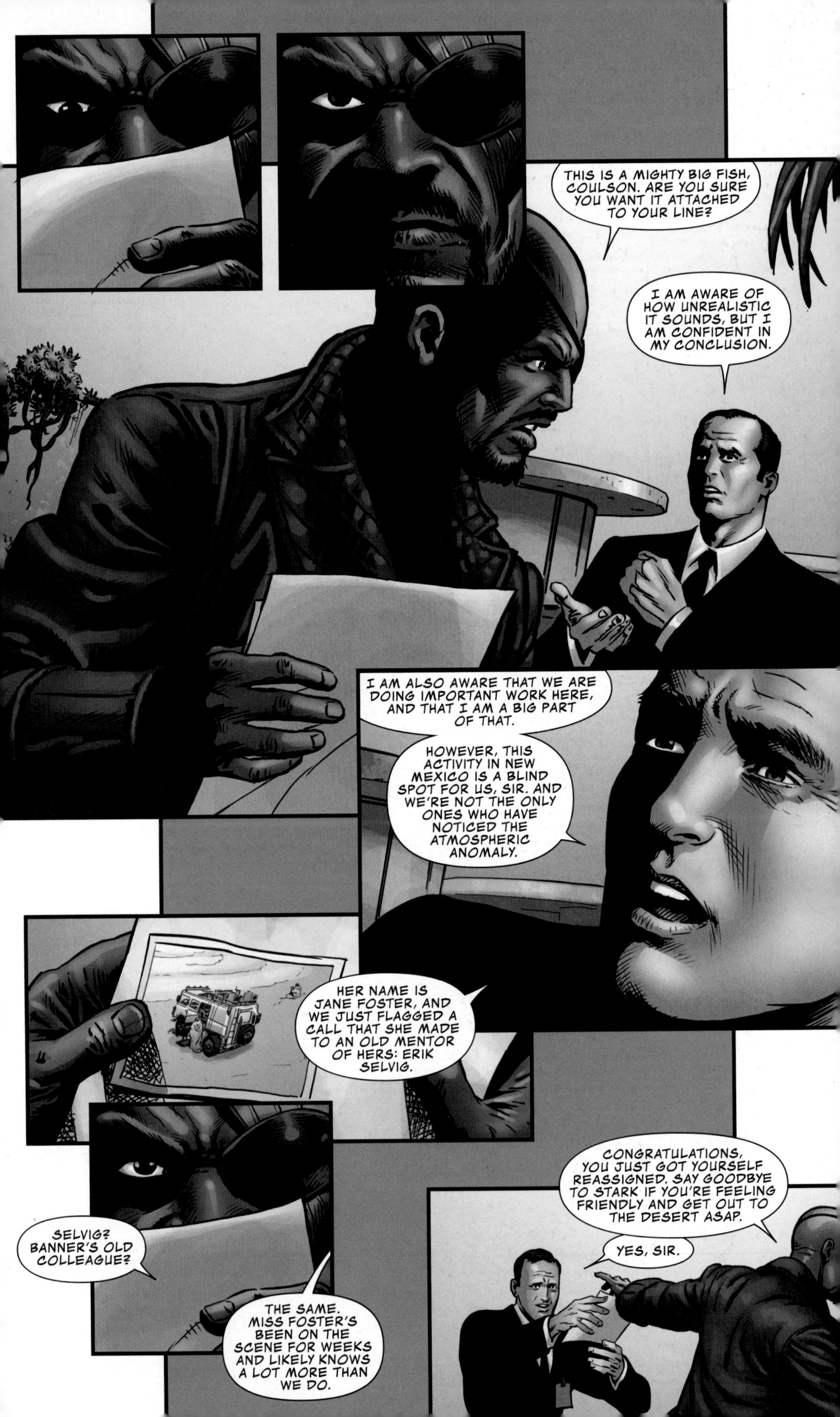
THIS IS A MIGHTY BIG FISH, COULSON. ARE YOU SURE YOU WANT IT ATTACHED TO YOUR LINE?
I AM AWARE OF HOW UNREALISTIC IT SOUNDS, BUT I AM CONFIDENT IN MY CONCLUSION.
I AM ALSO AWARE THAT WE ARE DOING IMPORTANT WORK HERE, AND THAT I AM A BIG PART OF THAT.
HOWEVER, THIS ACTIVITY IN NEW MEXICO IS A BLIND SPOT FOR US, SIR. AND WE'RE NOT THE ONLY ONES WHO HAVE NOTICED THE ATMOSPHERIC ANOMALY.
HER NAME IS JANE FOSTER, AND WE JUST FLAGGED A CALL THAT SHE MADE TO AN OLD MENTOR OF HERS: ERIK SELVIG.
SELVIG? BANNER'S OLD COLLEAGUE?
THE SAME. MISS FOSTER'S BEEN ON THE SCENE FOR WEEKS AND LIKELY KNOWS A LOT MORE THAN WE DO.
CONGRATULATIONS, YOU JUST GOT YOURSELF REASSIGNED. SAY GOODBYE TO STARK IF YOU'RE FEELING FRIENDLY AND GET OUT TO THE DESERT ASAP.
YES, SIR.

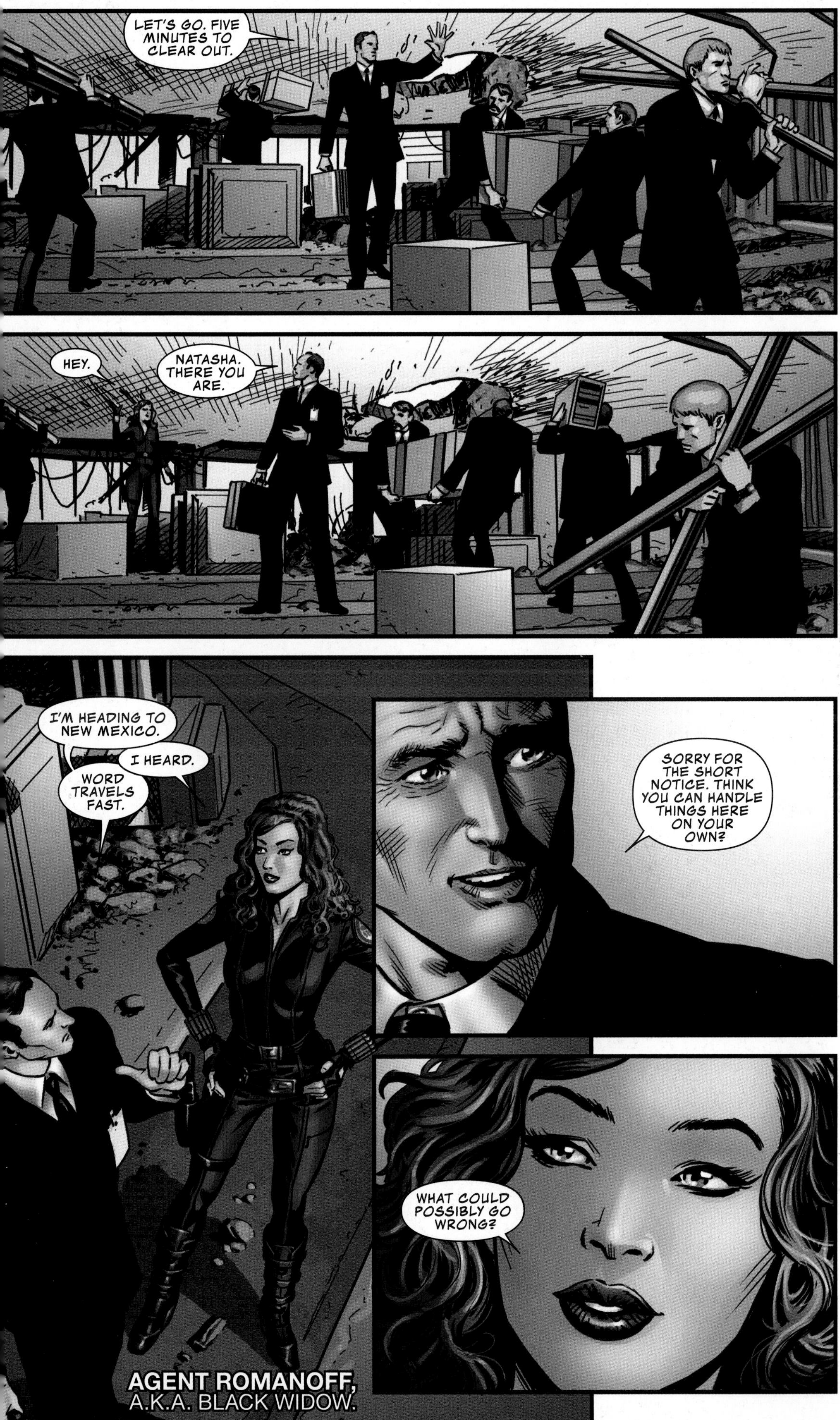
LET'S GO. FIVE MINUTES TO CLEAR OUT.
HEY.
NATASHA. THERE YOU ARE.
I'M HEADING TO NEW MEXICO.
I HEARD.
WORD TRAVELS FAST.
SORRY FOR THE SHORT NOTICE. THINK YOU CAN HANDLE THINGS HERE ON YOUR OWN?
WHAT COULD POSSIBLY GO WRONG?
AGENT ROMANOFF,
A.K.A. BLACK WIDOW.

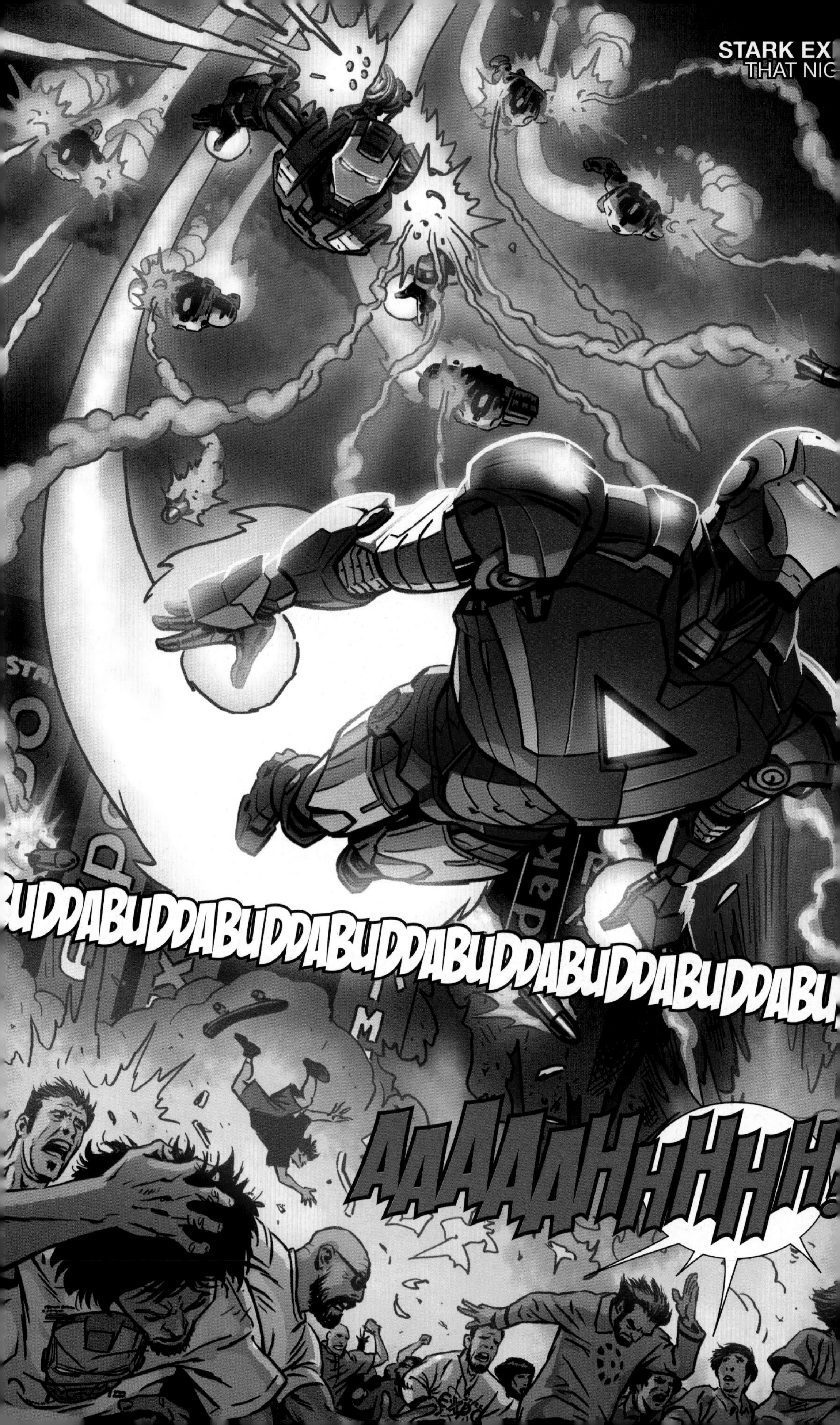
STARK EXI
THAT NIG
UDDABUDDABUDDABUDDABUDDABUDDABUDDABU
AAAAAHHHHH

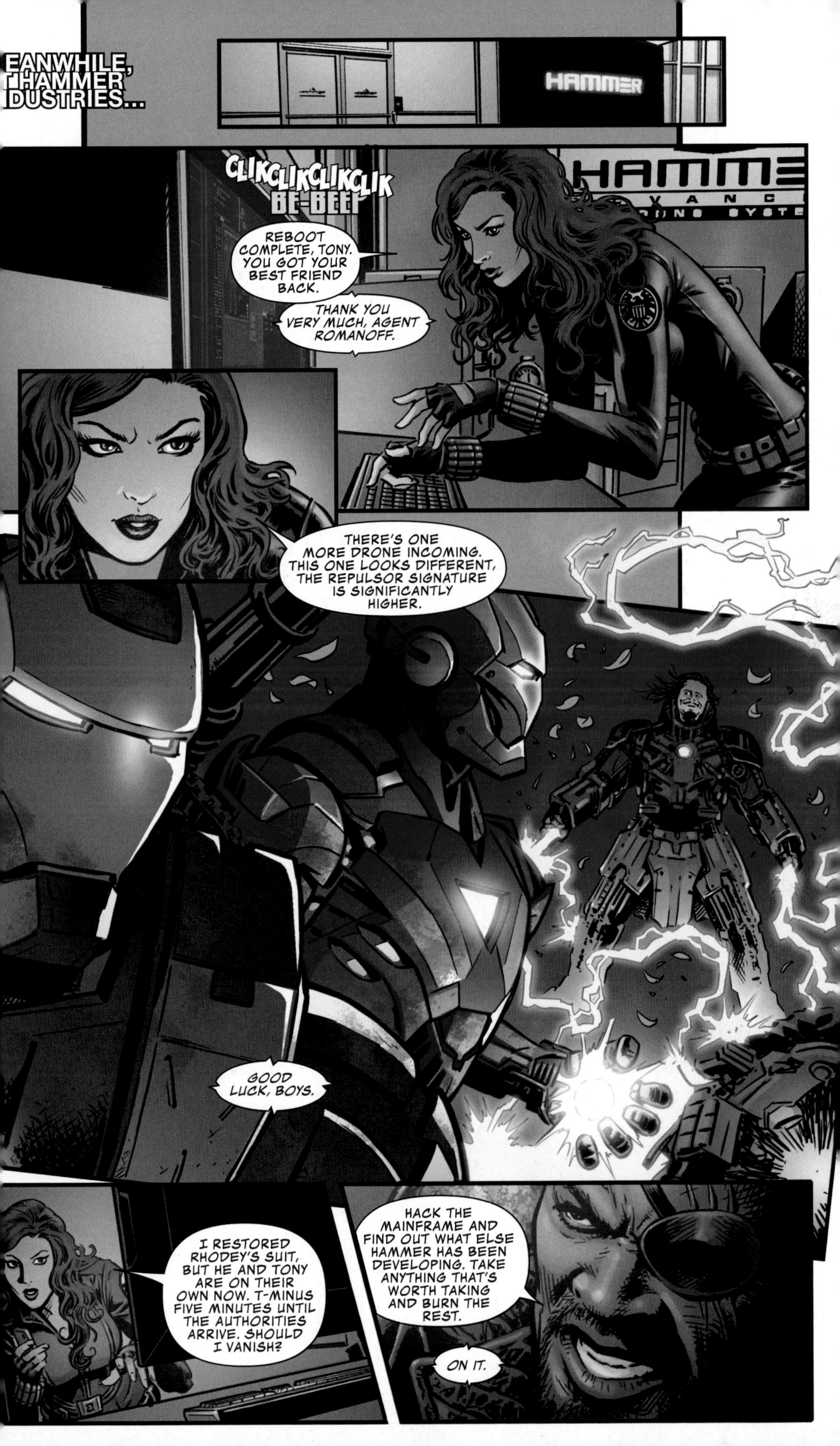
EANWHILE,
THAMMER
DUSTRIES...
HAMMER
CLIKCLIKCLIKCLIK
BE-BEEP
REBOOT COMPLETE, TONY. YOU GOT YOUR BEST FRIEND BACK.
THANK YOU VERY MUCH, AGENT ROMANOFF.
THERE'S ONE MORE DRONE INCOMING. THIS ONE LOOKS DIFFERENT. THE REPULSOR SIGNATURE IS SIGNIFICANTLY HIGHER.
GOOD LUCK, BOYS.
I RESTORED RHODEY'S SUIT, BUT HE AND TONY ARE ON THEIR OWN NOW. T-MINUS FIVE MINUTES UNTIL THE AUTHORITIES ARRIVE. SHOULD I VANISH?
HACK THE MAINFRAME AND FIND OUT WHAT ELSE HAMMER HAS BEEN DEVELOPING. TAKE ANYTHING THAT'S WORTH TAKING AND BURN THE REST.
ON IT.

INITIATING DOWNLOAD...

BEEP

COUNTDOWN INITIATED.

00:05:

PROTOTYPES

00:04:00

DISGUSTING...

00:03:0

00:02:00

DOWNLOAD COMPLETE.

00:01:0

HAMMER

POLICE

WEOOWEOOWEOOWEOOWEOOWEOO

00:00:00

BOOM

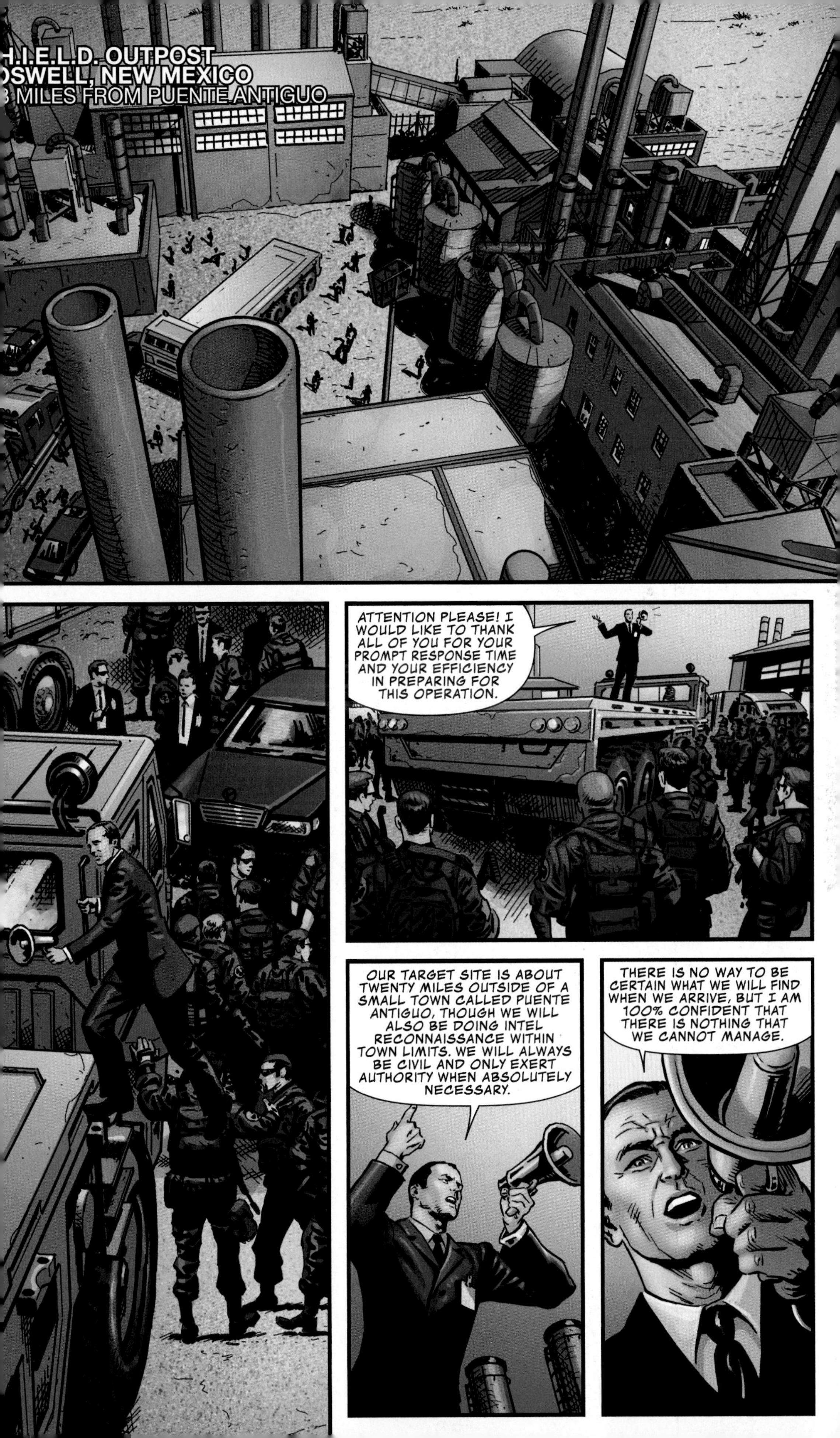
H.I.E.L.D. OUTPOST
OSWELL, NEW MEXICO
3 MILES FROM PUENTE ANTIGUO
ATTENTION PLEASE! I WOULD LIKE TO THANK ALL OF YOU FOR YOUR PROMPT RESPONSE TIME AND YOUR EFFICIENCY IN PREPARING FOR THIS OPERATION.
OUR TARGET SITE IS ABOUT TWENTY MILES OUTSIDE OF A SMALL TOWN CALLED PUENTE ANTIGUO, THOUGH WE WILL ALSO BE DOING INTEL RECONNAISSANCE WITHIN TOWN LIMITS. WE WILL ALWAYS BE CIVIL AND ONLY EXERT AUTHORITY WHEN ABSOLUTELY NECESSARY.
THERE IS NO WAY TO BE CERTAIN WHAT WE WILL FIND WHEN WE ARRIVE, BUT I AM 100% CONFIDENT THAT THERE IS NOTHING THAT WE CANNOT MANAGE.

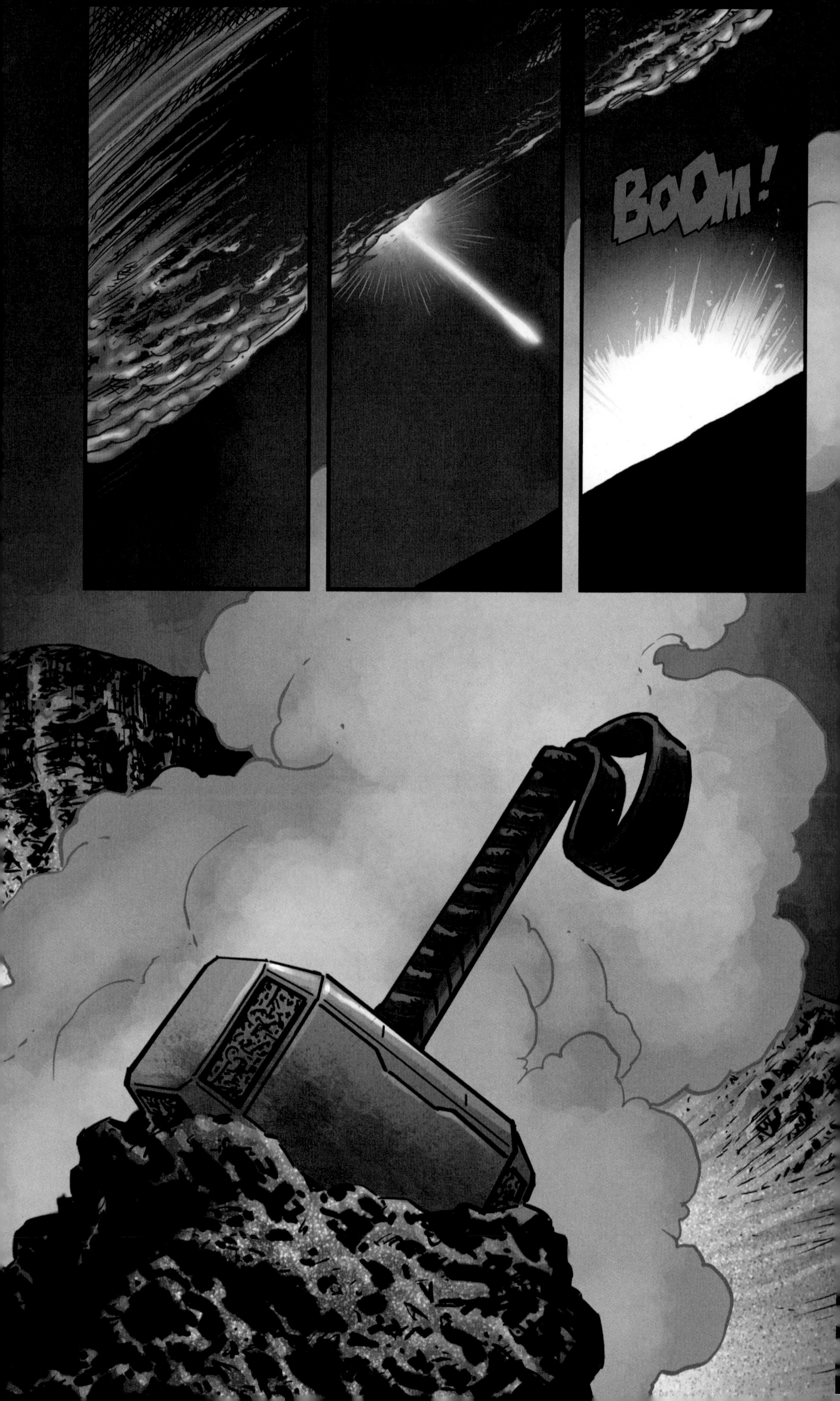
BOOM!

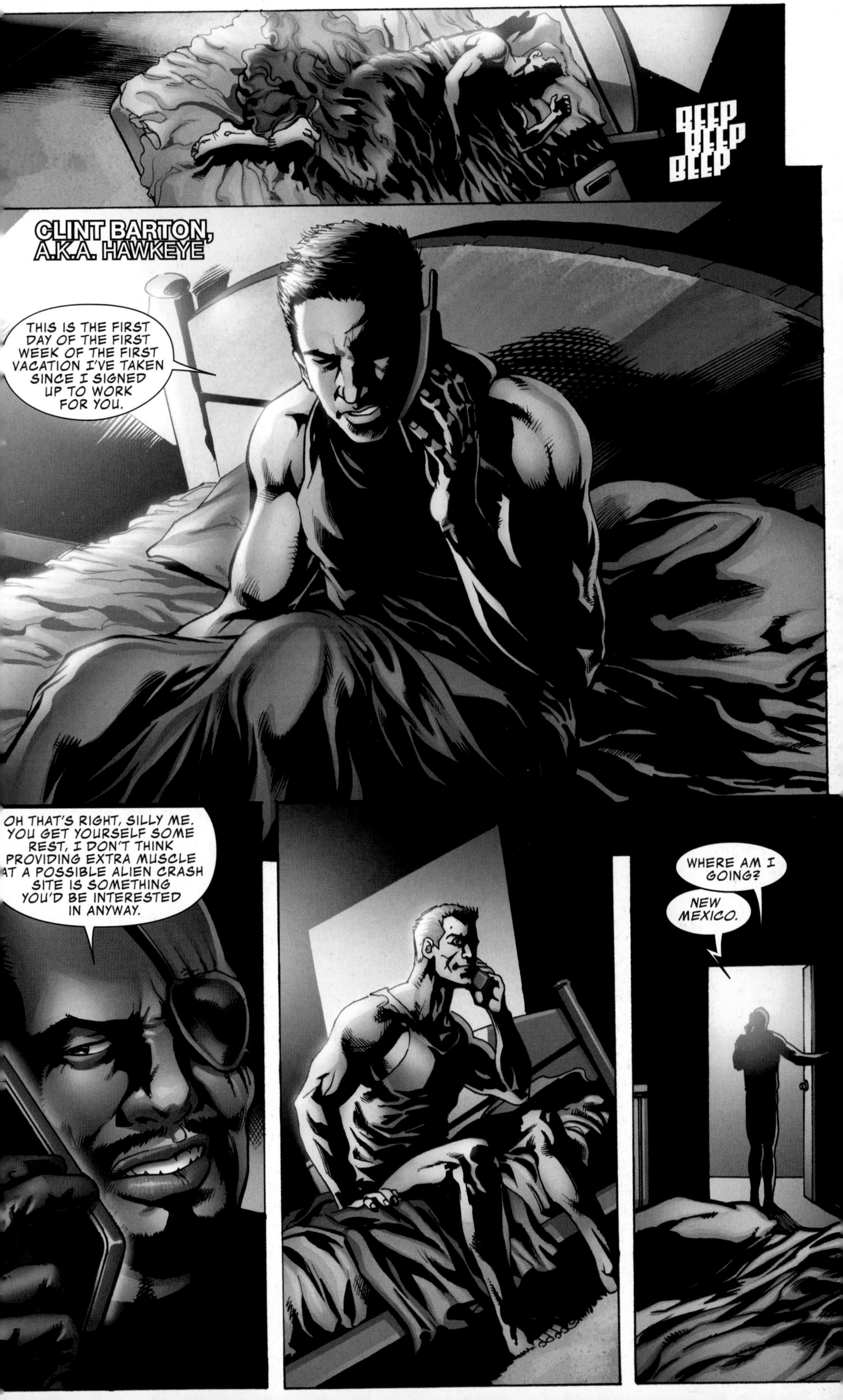
BEEP
BEEP
BEEP
CLINT BARTON, A.K.A. HAWKEYE
THIS IS THE FIRST DAY OF THE FIRST WEEK OF THE FIRST VACATION I'VE TAKEN SINCE I SIGNED UP TO WORK FOR YOU.
OH THAT'S RIGHT, SILLY ME. YOU GET YOURSELF SOME REST, I DON'T THINK PROVIDING EXTRA MUSCLE AT A POSSIBLE ALIEN CRASH SITE IS SOMETHING YOU'D BE INTERESTED IN ANYWAY.
WHERE AM I GOING?
NEW MEXICO.

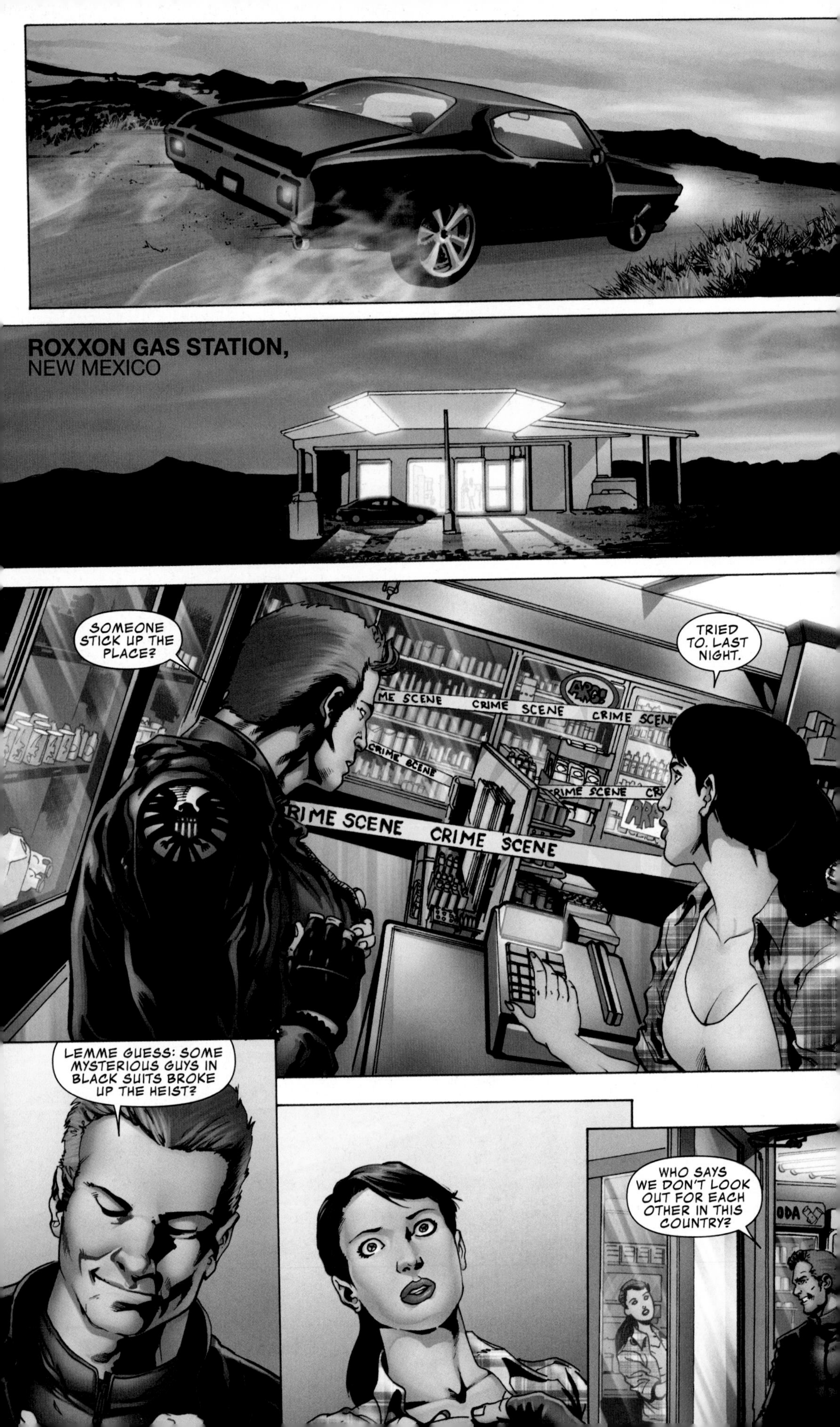
ROXXON GAS STATION,
NEW MEXICO
SOMEONE STICK UP THE PLACE?
TRIED TO. LAST NIGHT.
CRIME SCENE
LEMME GUESS: SOME MYSTERIOUS GUYS IN BLACK SUITS BROKE UP THE HEIST?
WHO SAYS WE DON'T LOOK OUT FOR EACH OTHER IN THIS COUNTRY?

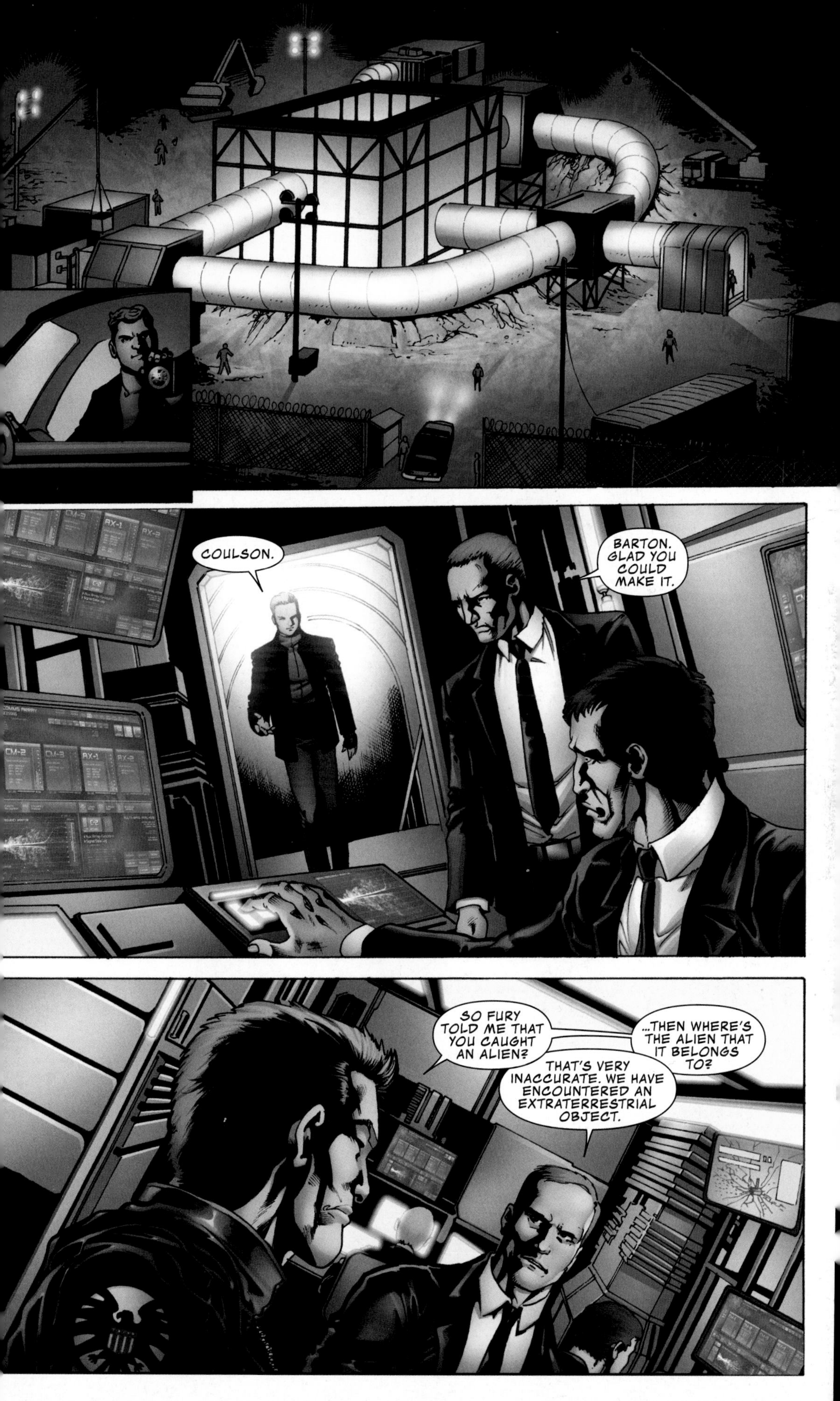
COULSON.
BARTON. GLAD YOU COULD MAKE IT.
SO FURY TOLD ME THAT YOU CAUGHT AN ALIEN?
THAT'S VERY INACCURATE. WE HAVE ENCOUNTERED AN EXTRATERRESTRIAL OBJECT.
...THEN WHERE'S THE ALIEN THAT IT BELONGS TO?

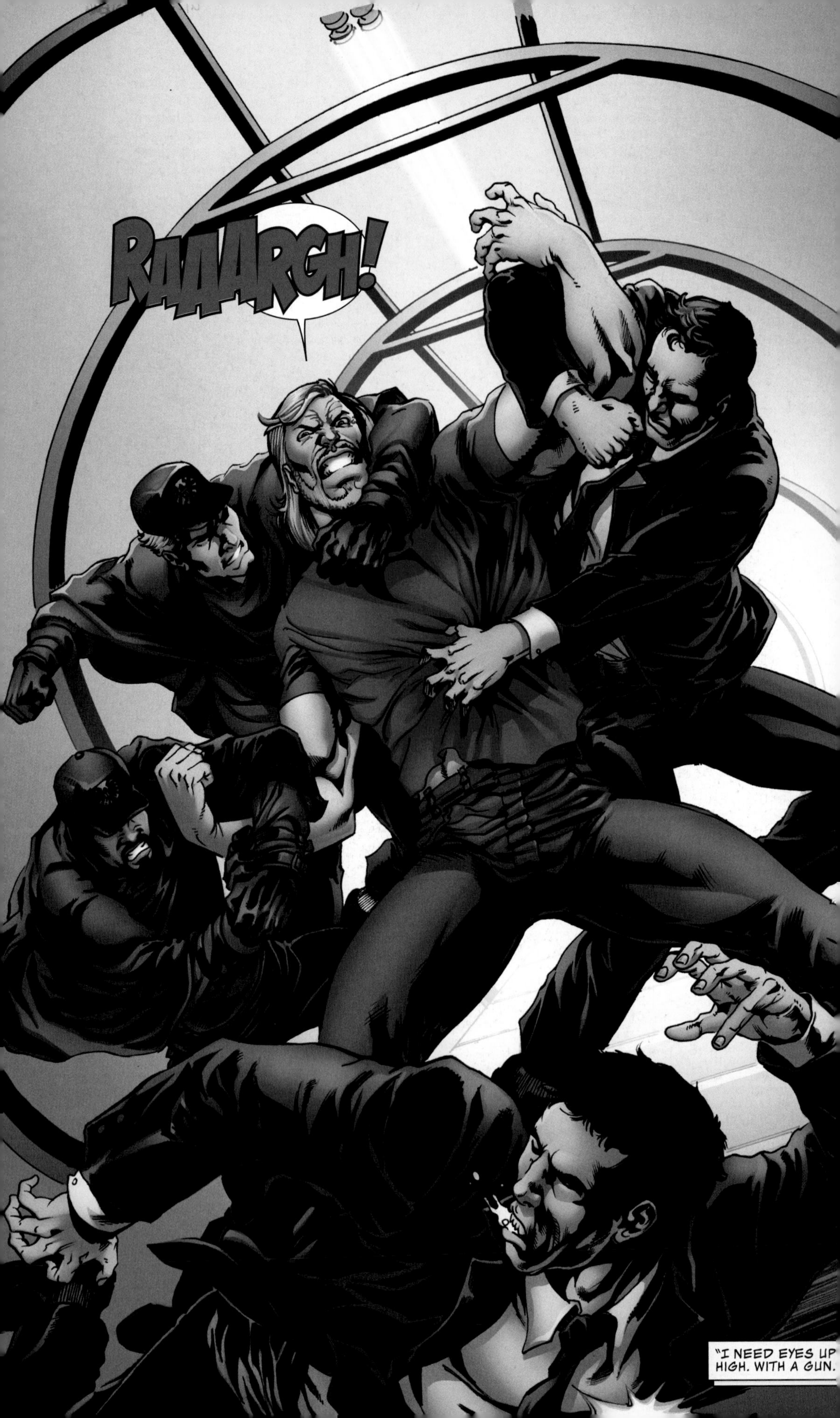
RAAARGH!
"I NEED EYES UP HIGH. WITH A GUN.

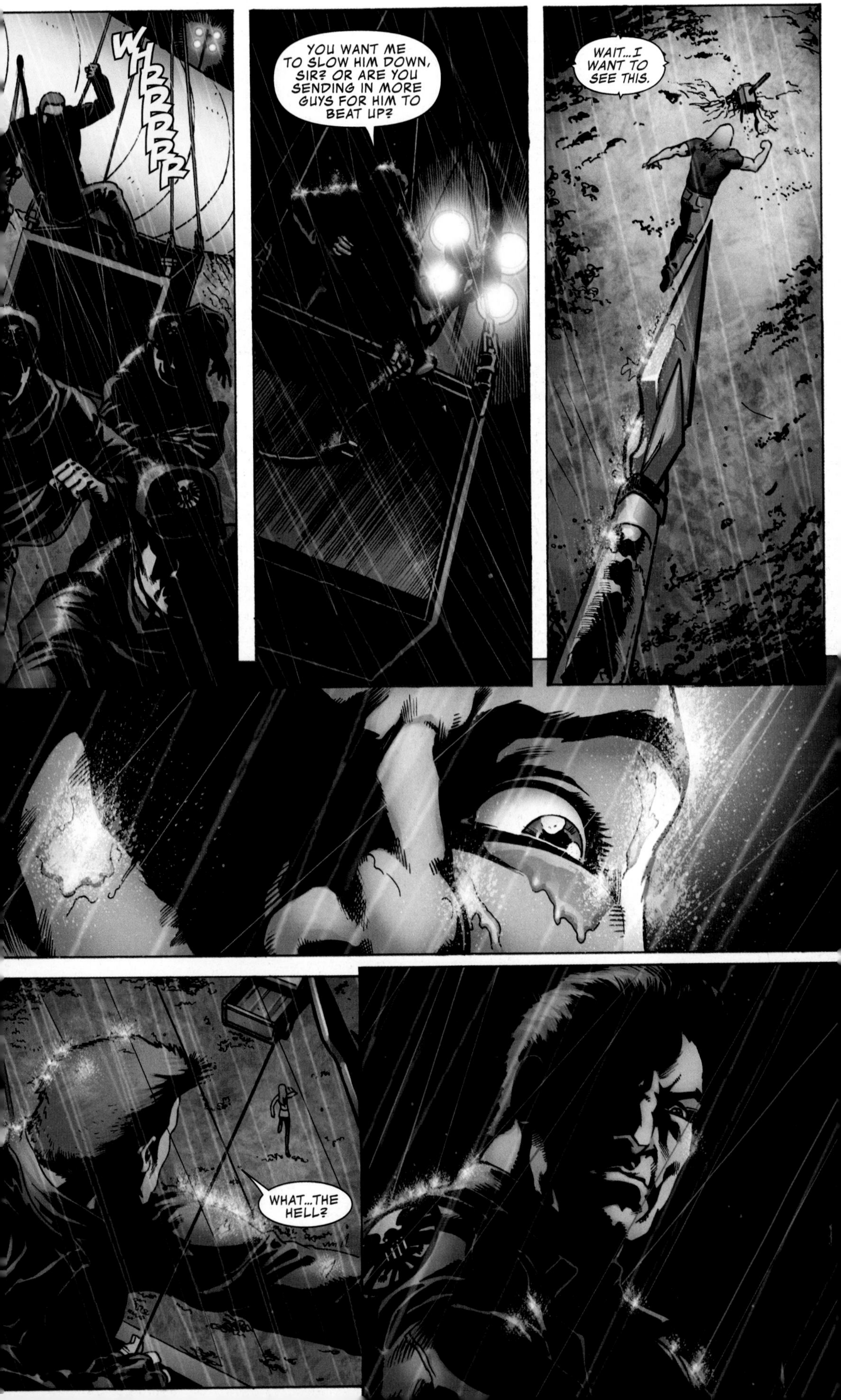
WHRRRR
YOU WANT ME TO SLOW HIM DOWN, SIR? OR ARE YOU SENDING IN MORE GUYS FOR HIM TO BEAT UP?
WAIT...I WANT TO SEE THIS.
WHAT...THE HELL?

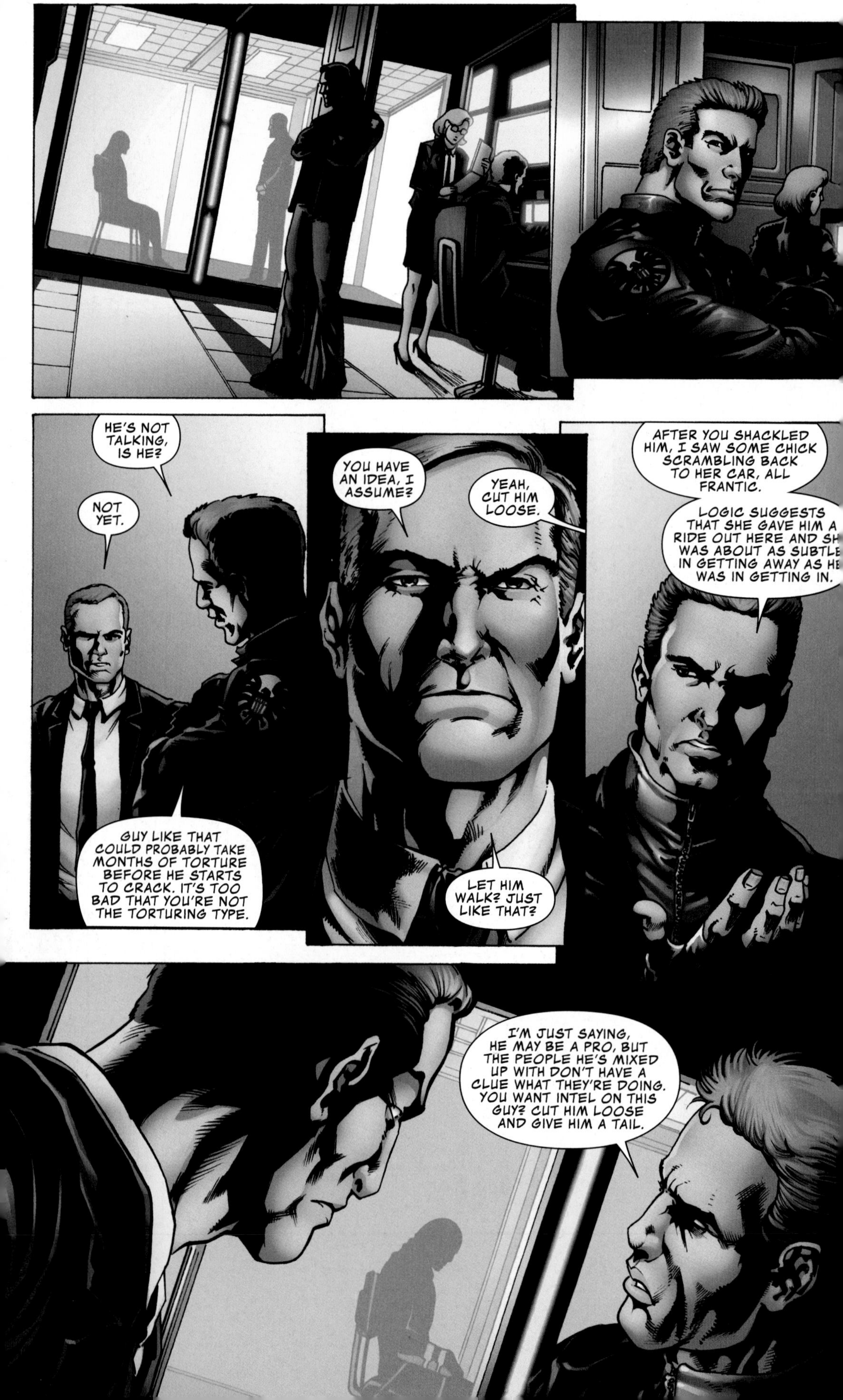
HE'S NOT TALKING, IS HE?
NOT YET.
GUY LIKE THAT COULD PROBABLY TAKE MONTHS OF TORTURE BEFORE HE STARTS TO CRACK. IT'S TOO BAD THAT YOU'RE NOT THE TORTURING TYPE.
YOU HAVE AN IDEA, I ASSUME?
YEAH, CUT HIM LOOSE.
LET HIM WALK? JUST LIKE THAT?
AFTER YOU SHACKLED HIM, I SAW SOME CHICK SCRAMBLING BACK TO HER CAR, ALL FRANTIC.
LOGIC SUGGESTS THAT SHE GAVE HIM A RIDE OUT HERE AND SH WAS ABOUT AS SUBTLE IN GETTING AWAY AS HE WAS IN GETTING IN.
I'M JUST SAYING, HE MAY BE A PRO, BUT THE PEOPLE HE'S MIXED UP WITH DON'T HAVE A CLUE WHAT THEY'RE DOING. YOU WANT INTEL ON THIS GUY? CUT HIM LOOSE AND GIVE HIM A TAIL.

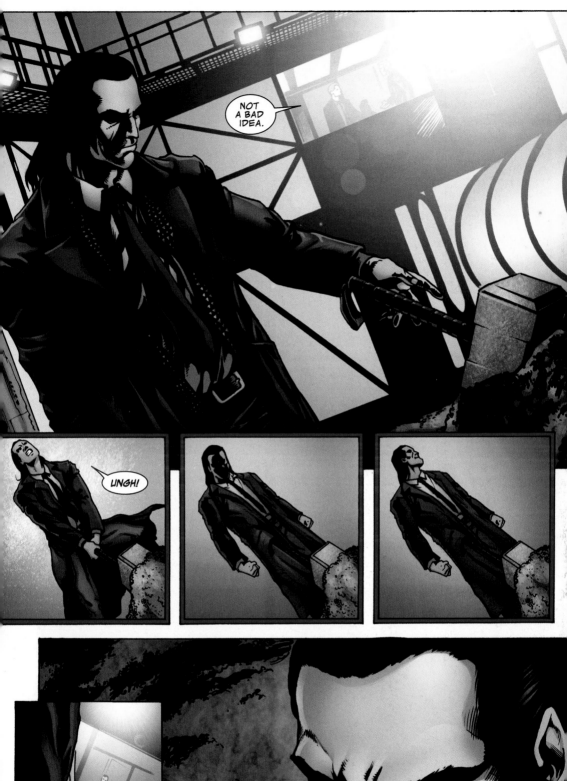

NOT A BAD IDEA.

UNGH!

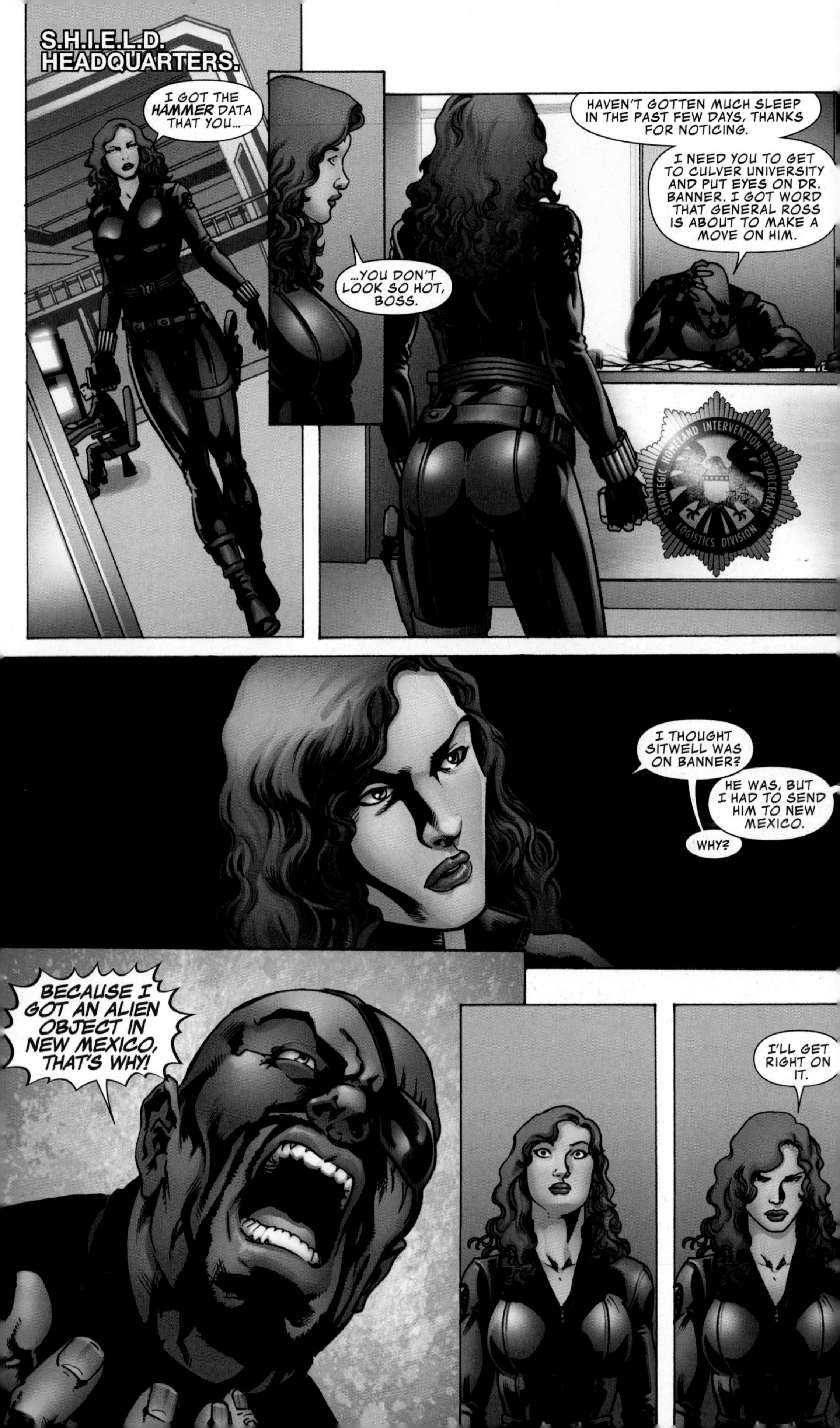
S.H.I.E.L.D. HEADQUARTERS.
I GOT THE HAMMER DATA THAT YOU...
...YOU DON'T LOOK SO HOT, BOSS.
HAVEN'T GOTTEN MUCH SLEEP IN THE PAST FEW DAYS, THANKS FOR NOTICING.
I NEED YOU TO GET TO CULVER UNIVERSITY AND PUT EYES ON DR. BANNER. I GOT WORD THAT GENERAL ROSS IS ABOUT TO MAKE A MOVE ON HIM.
STRATEGIC HOMELAND INTERVENTION ENFORCEMENT LOGISTICS DIVISION
I THOUGHT SITWELL WAS ON BANNER?
HE WAS, BUT I HAD TO SEND HIM TO NEW MEXICO.
WHY?
BECAUSE I GOT AN ALIEN OBJECT IN NEW MEXICO, THAT'S WHY!
I'LL GET RIGHT ON IT.

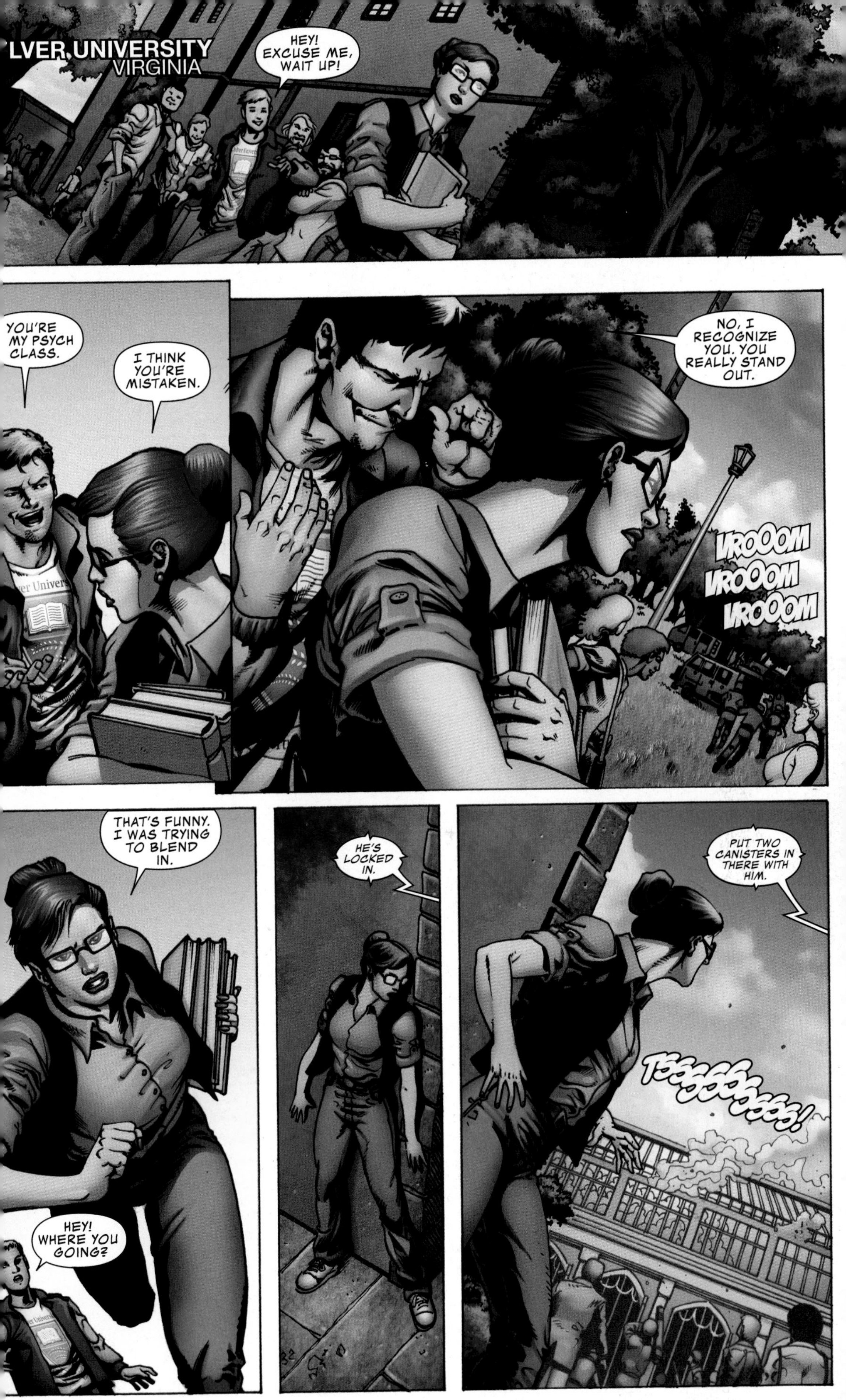
LVER UNIVERSITY
VIRGINIA
HEY! EXCUSE ME, WAIT UP!
YOU'RE MY PSYCH CLASS.
I THINK YOU'RE MISTAKEN.
NO, I RECOGNIZE YOU. YOU REALLY STAND OUT.
VROOOM VROOOM VROOOM
THAT'S FUNNY. I WAS TRYING TO BLEND IN.
HEY! WHERE YOU GOING?
HE'S LOCKED IN.
PUT TWO CANISTERS IN THERE WITH HIM.
TSSSSSSSSSS!

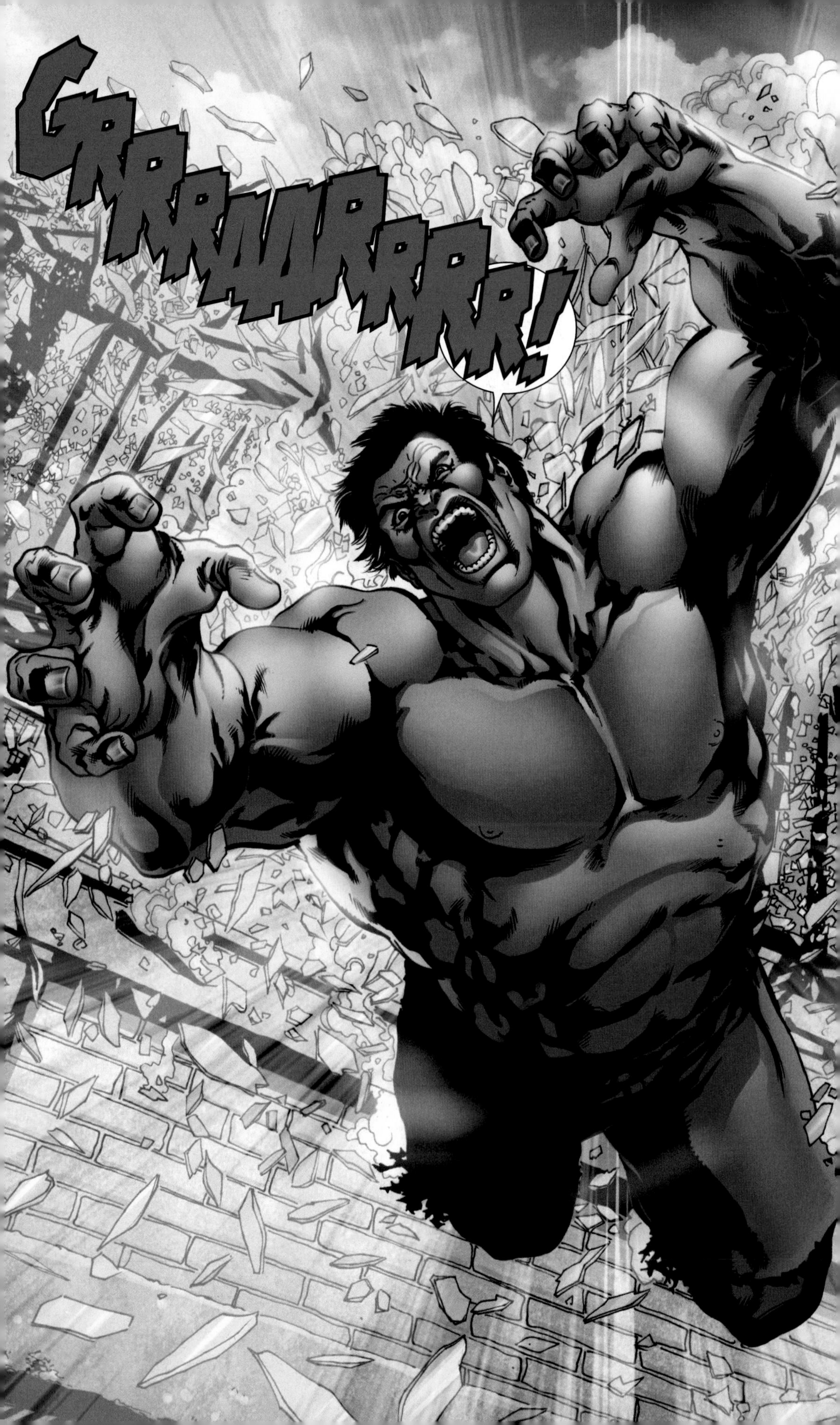
GRRRWWRRRRR!

STRATEGIC HOMELAND INTERVENTION ENFORCEMENT
LOGISTICS DIVISION

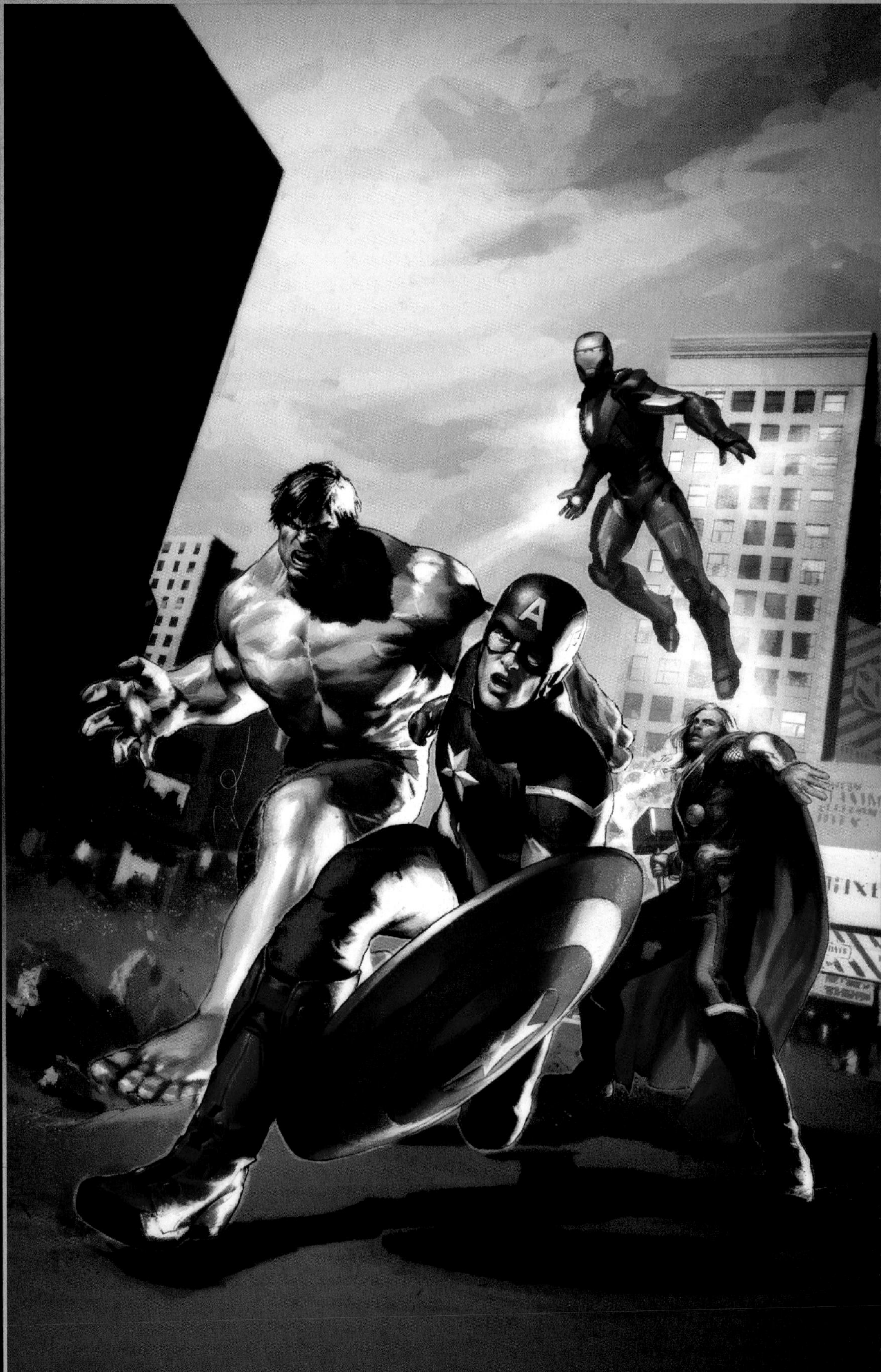

THREE

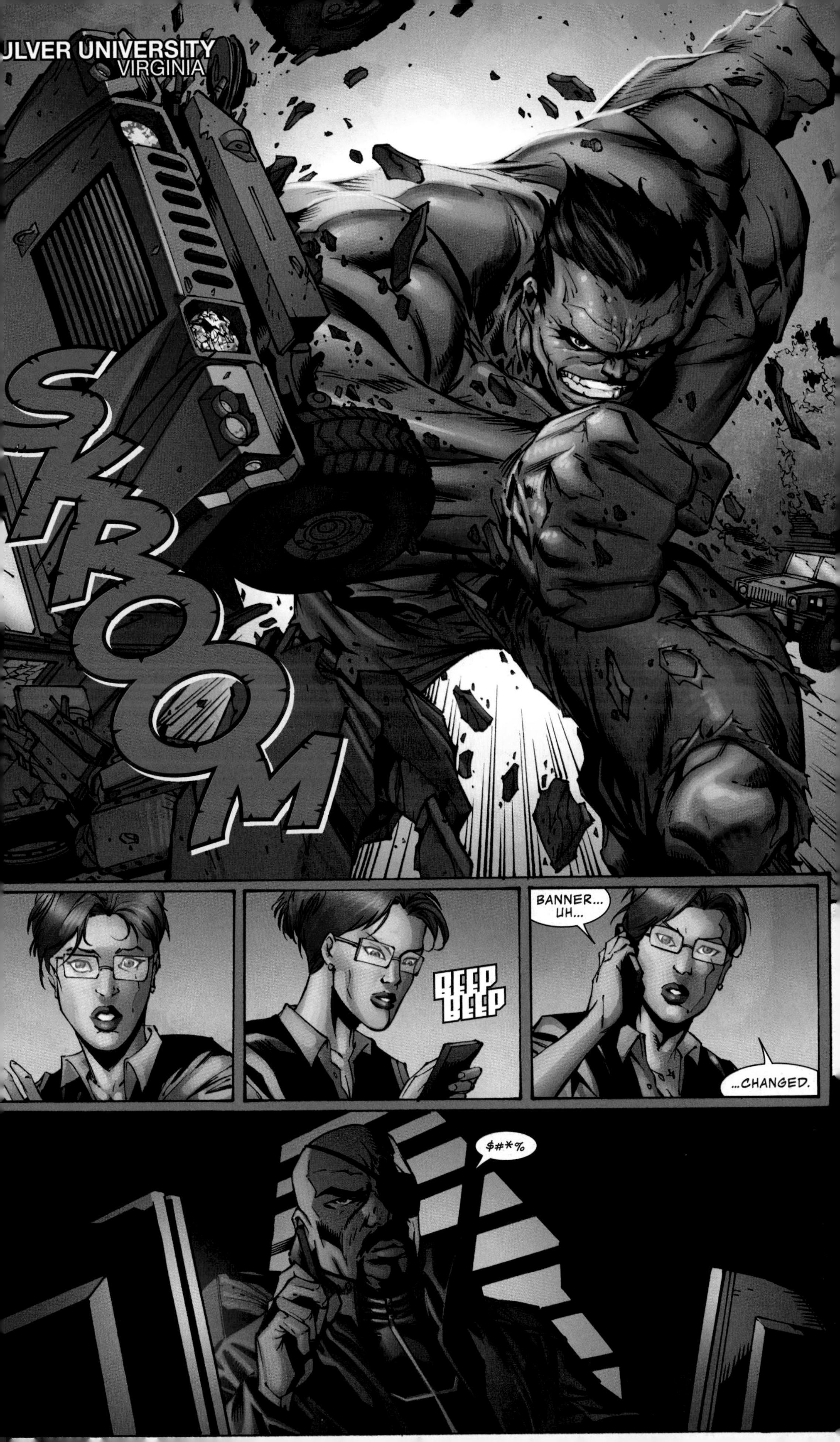

ULVER UNIVERSITY
VIRGINIA
SKROOM
BEEP BEEP
BANNER... UH...
...CHANGED.
$#*%

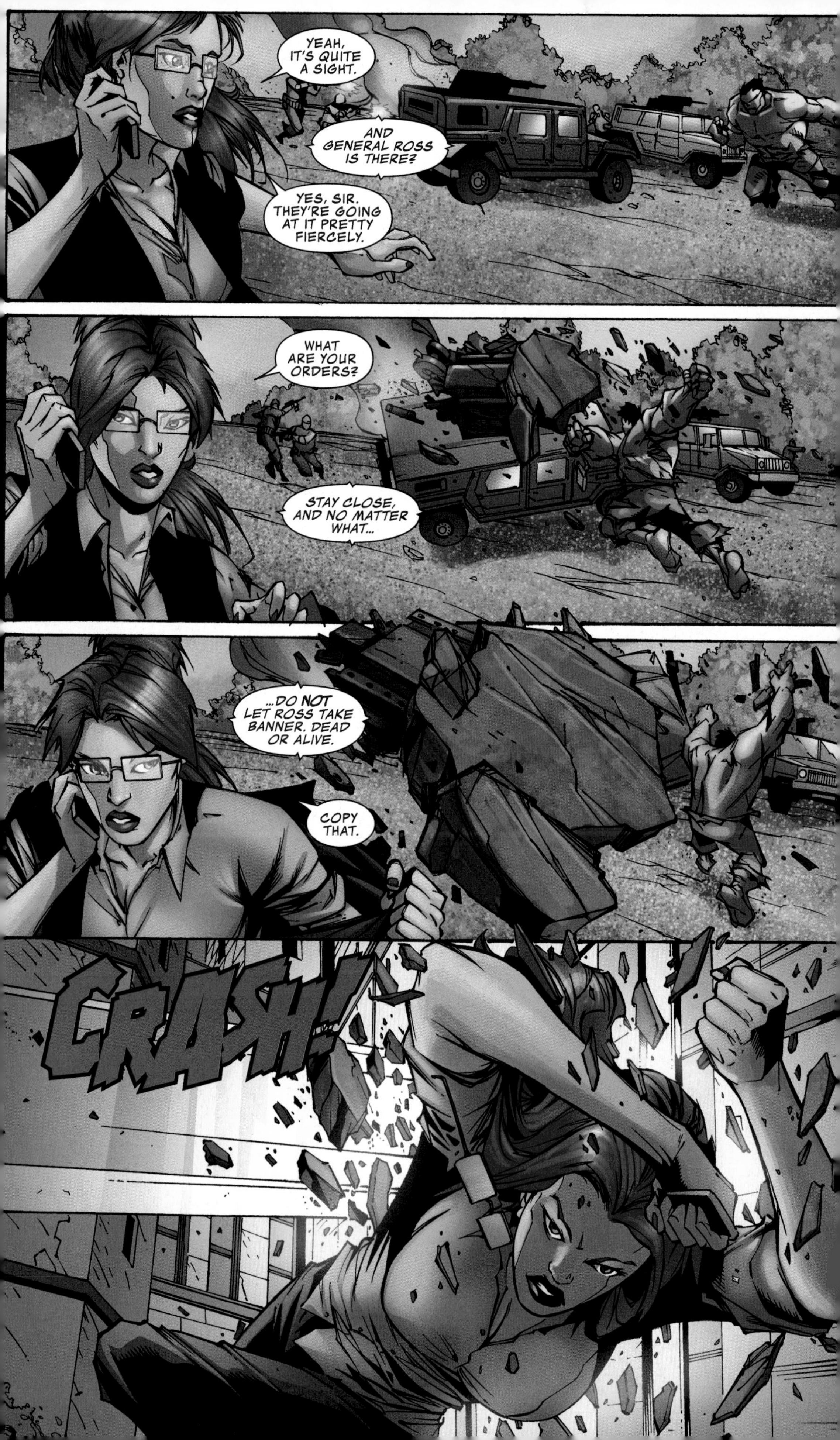
YEAH, IT'S QUITE A SIGHT.
AND GENERAL ROSS IS THERE?
YES, SIR. THEY'RE GOING AT IT PRETTY FIERCELY.
WHAT ARE YOUR ORDERS?
STAY CLOSE, AND NO MATTER WHAT...
...DO NOT LET ROSS TAKE BANNER. DEAD OR ALIVE.
COPY THAT.
CRASH!

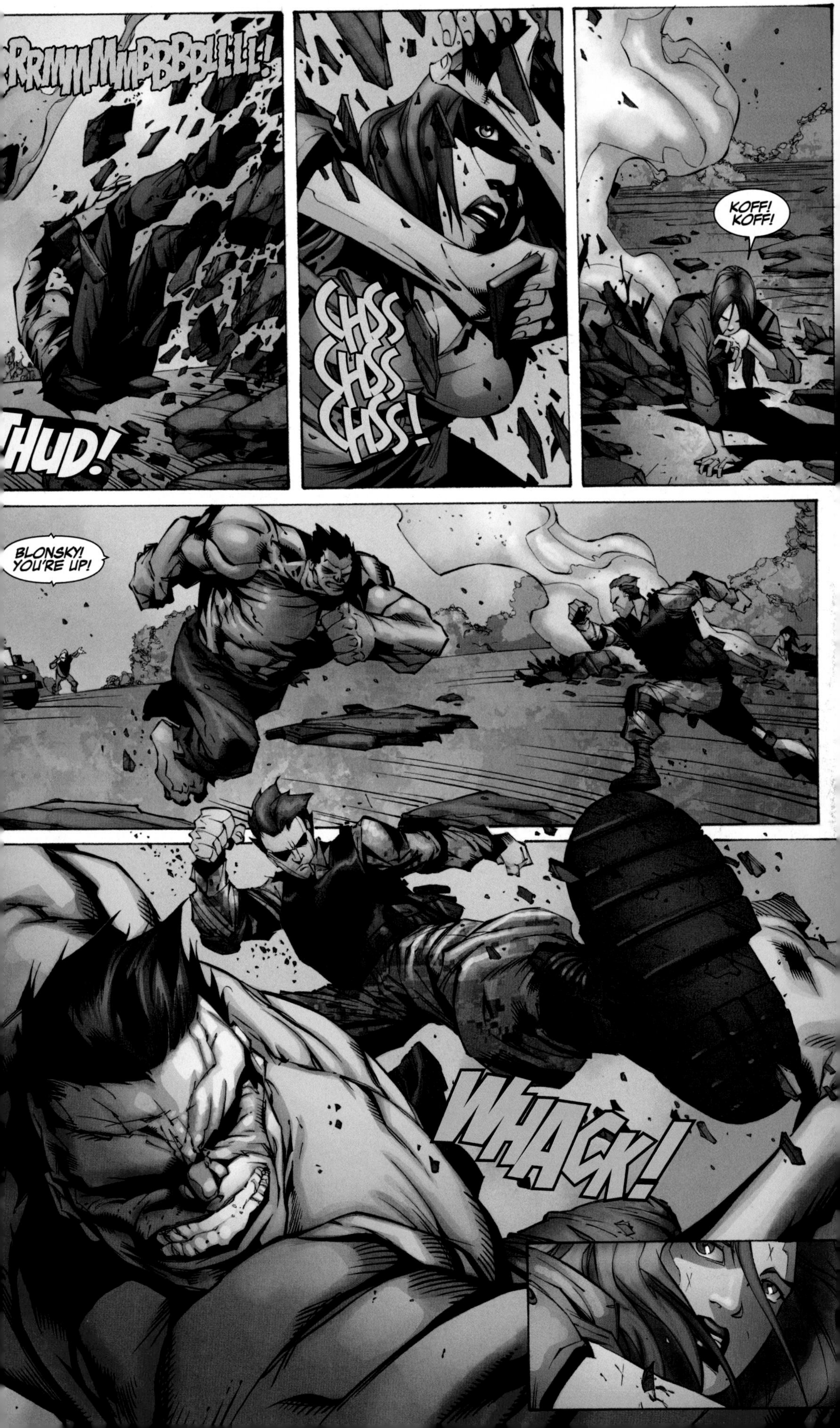
RRMMMMBBBLLLL!
THUD!
CHSS CHSS CHSS!
KOFF! KOFF!
BLONSKY! YOU'RE UP!
WHACK!

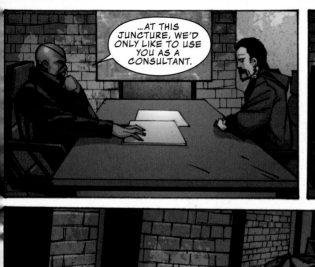

...AT THIS JUNCTURE, WE'D ONLY LIKE TO USE YOU AS A CONSULTANT.

WE NEED TO TALK.

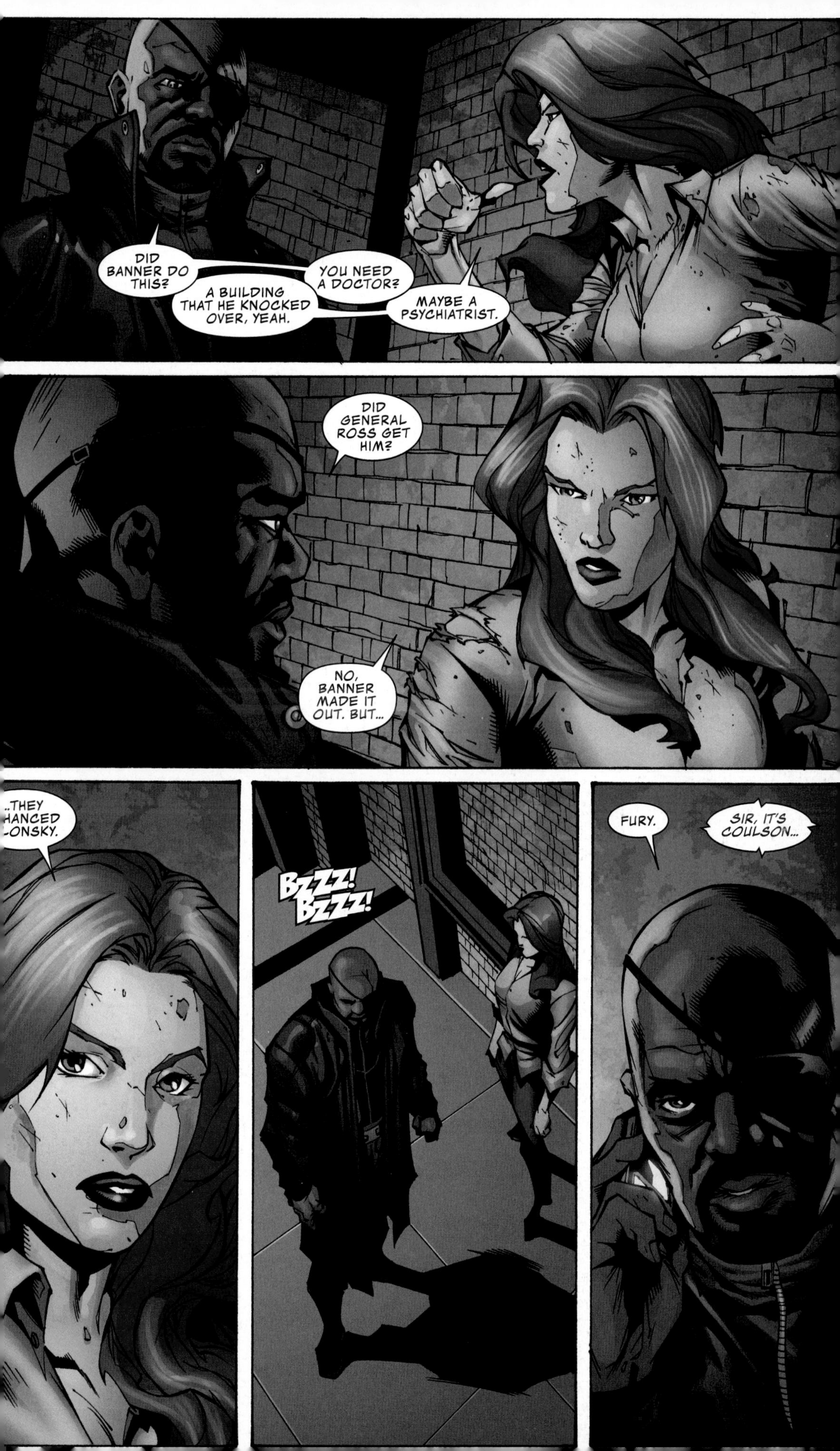
DID BANNER DO THIS?
YOU NEED A DOCTOR?
A BUILDING THAT HE KNOCKED OVER, YEAH.
MAYBE A PSYCHIATRIST.
DID GENERAL ROSS GET HIM?
NO, BANNER MADE IT OUT. BUT...
..THEY HANCED -ONSKY.
BZZZ! BZZZ!
FURY.
SIR, IT'S COULSON...

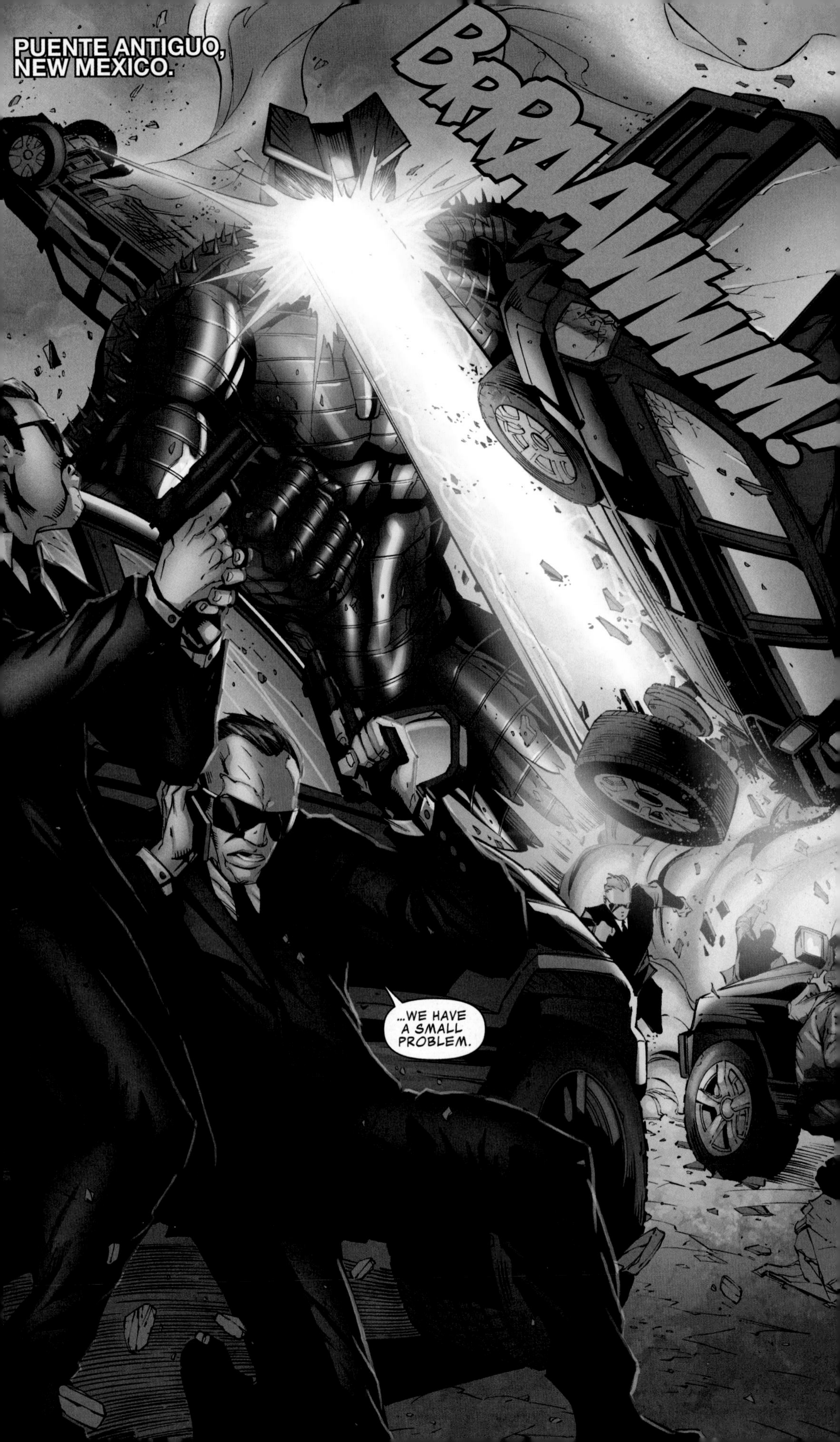
PUENTE ANTIGUO, NEW MEXICO.
BRRAMM!
...WE HAVE A SMALL PROBLEM.

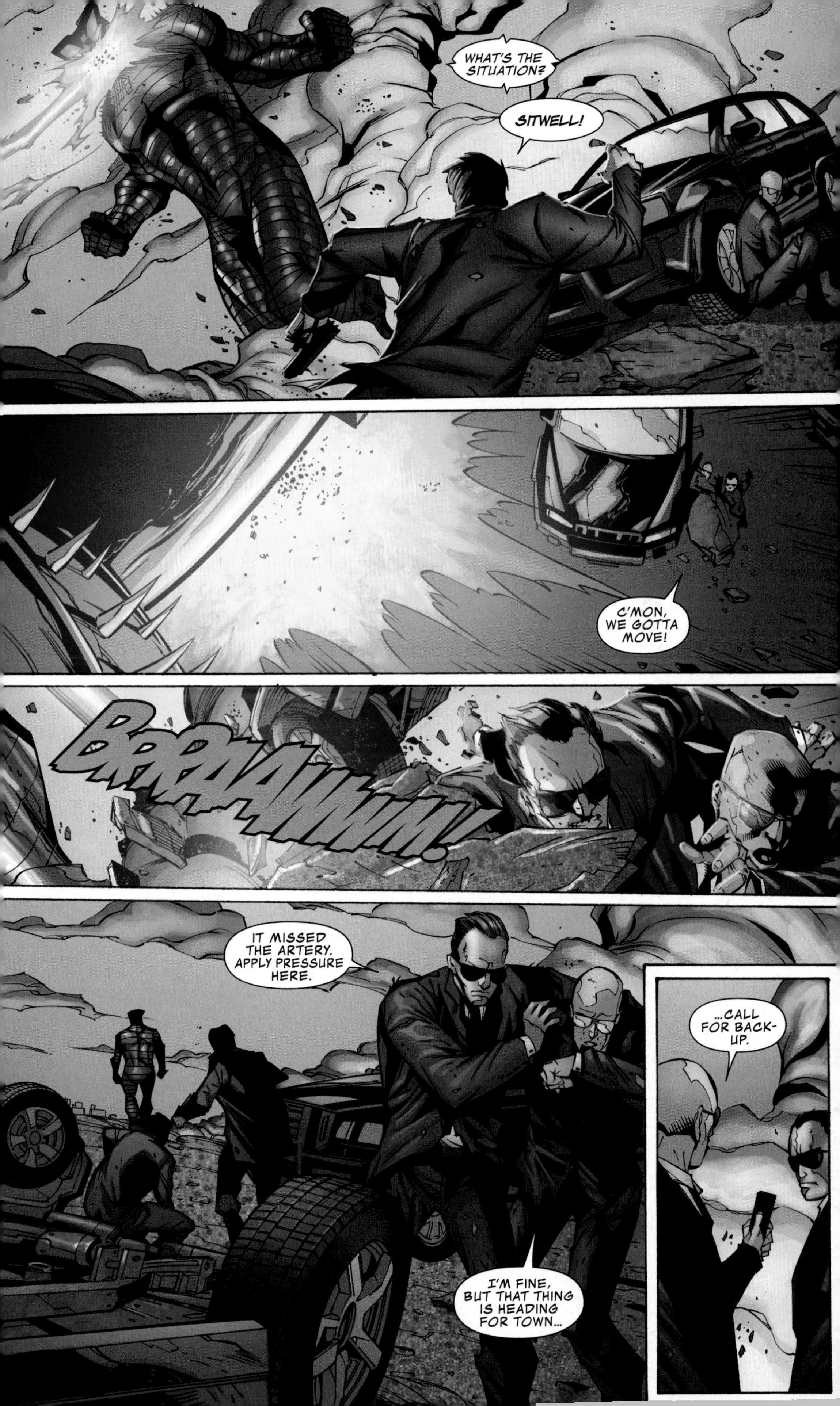
WHAT'S THE SITUATION?
SITWELL!
C'MON, WE GOTTA MOVE!
BRRRAWWWM!
IT MISSED THE ARTERY. APPLY PRESSURE HERE.
I'M FINE, BUT THAT THING IS HEADING FOR TOWN...
...CALL FOR BACK-UP.

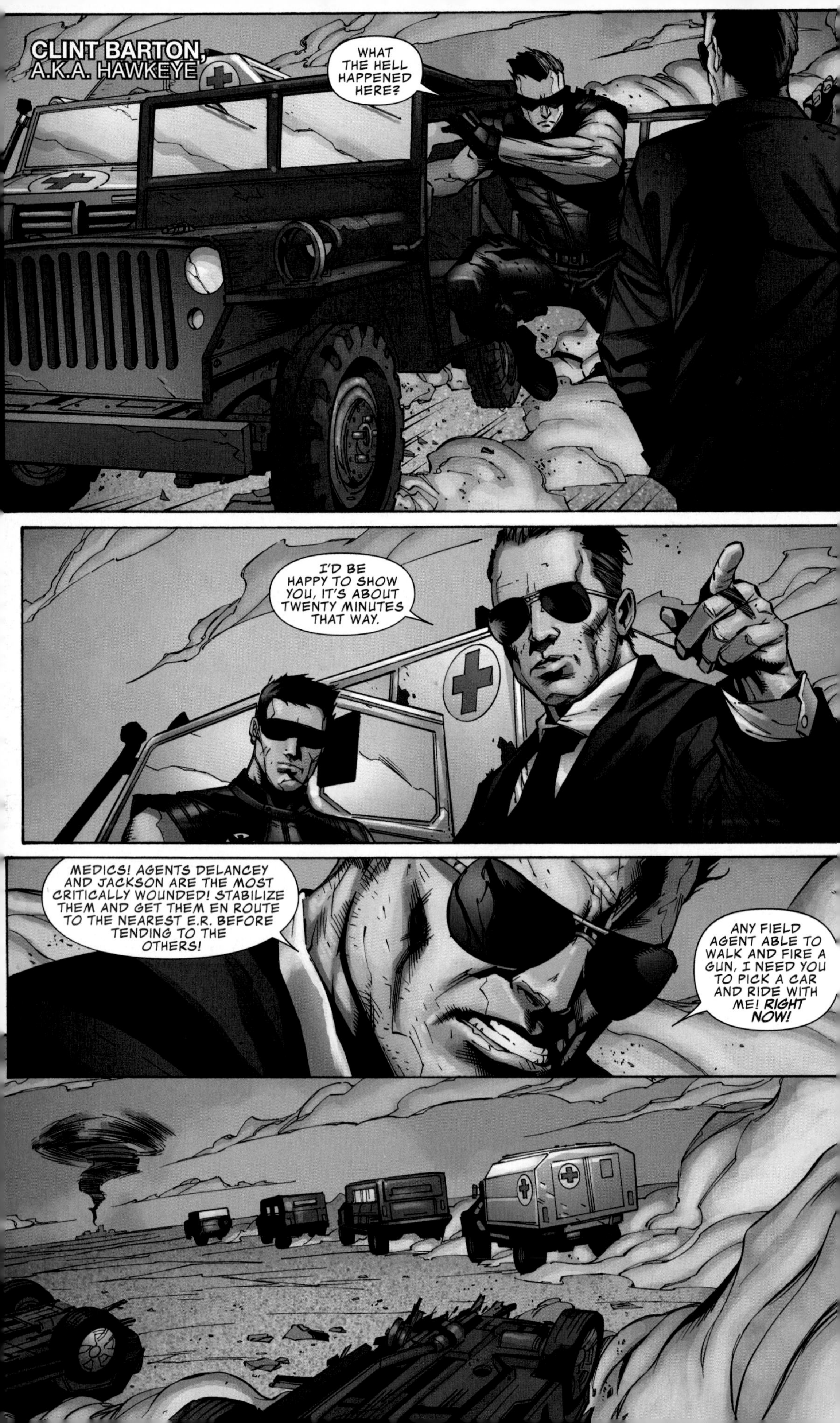

CLINT BARTON,
A.K.A. HAWKEYE
WHAT THE HELL HAPPENED HERE?
I'D BE HAPPY TO SHOW YOU, IT'S ABOUT TWENTY MINUTES THAT WAY.
MEDICS! AGENTS DELANCEY AND JACKSON ARE THE MOST CRITICALLY WOUNDED! STABILIZE THEM AND GET THEM EN ROUTE TO THE NEAREST E.R. BEFORE TENDING TO THE OTHERS!
ANY FIELD AGENT ABLE TO WALK AND FIRE A GUN, I NEED YOU TO PICK A CAR AND RIDE WITH ME! RIGHT NOW!

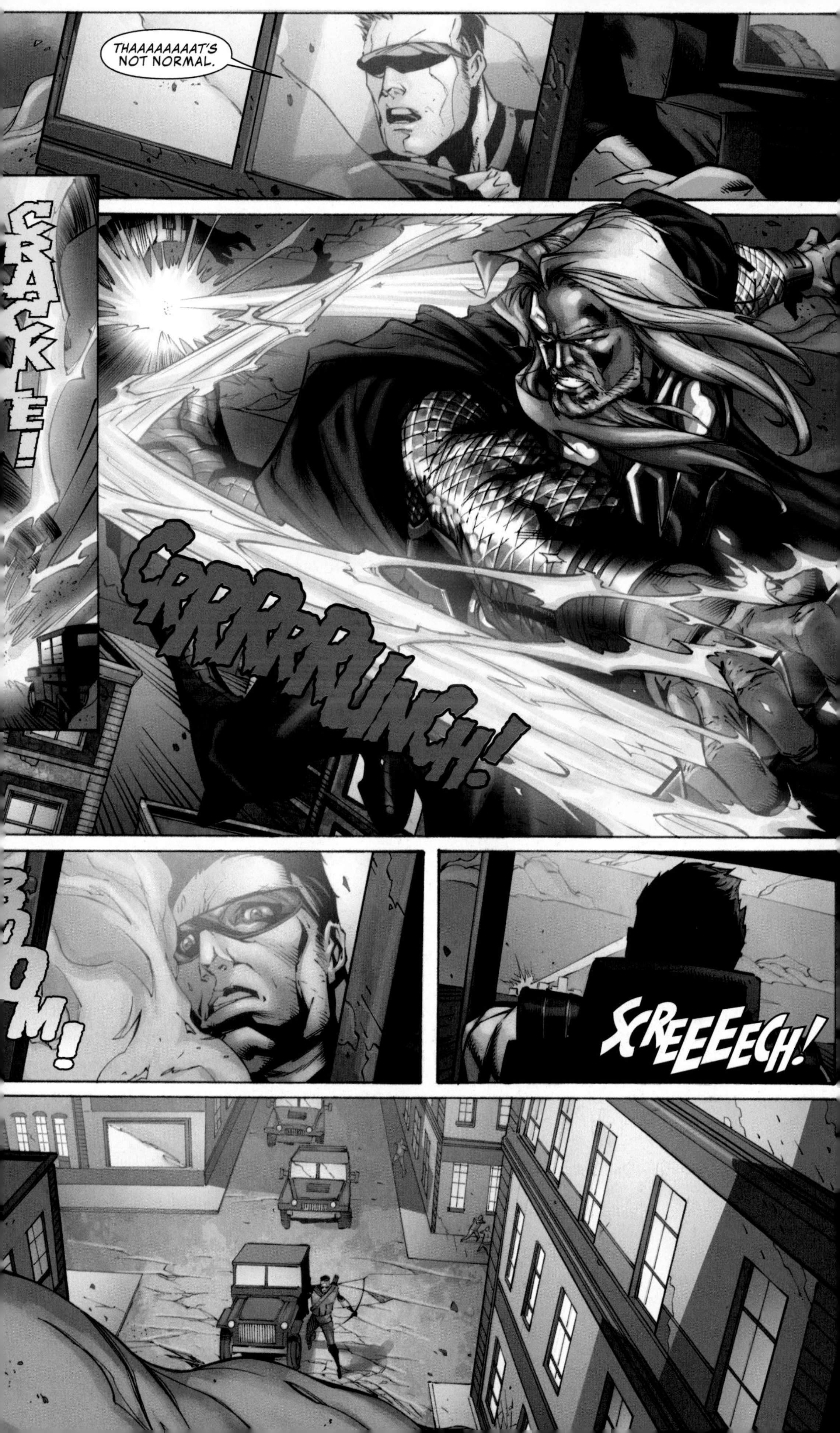
THAAAAAAAAT'S NOT NORMAL.
CRACKLE!
GRRRRRRUNCH!
BOOM!
SCREEEECH!

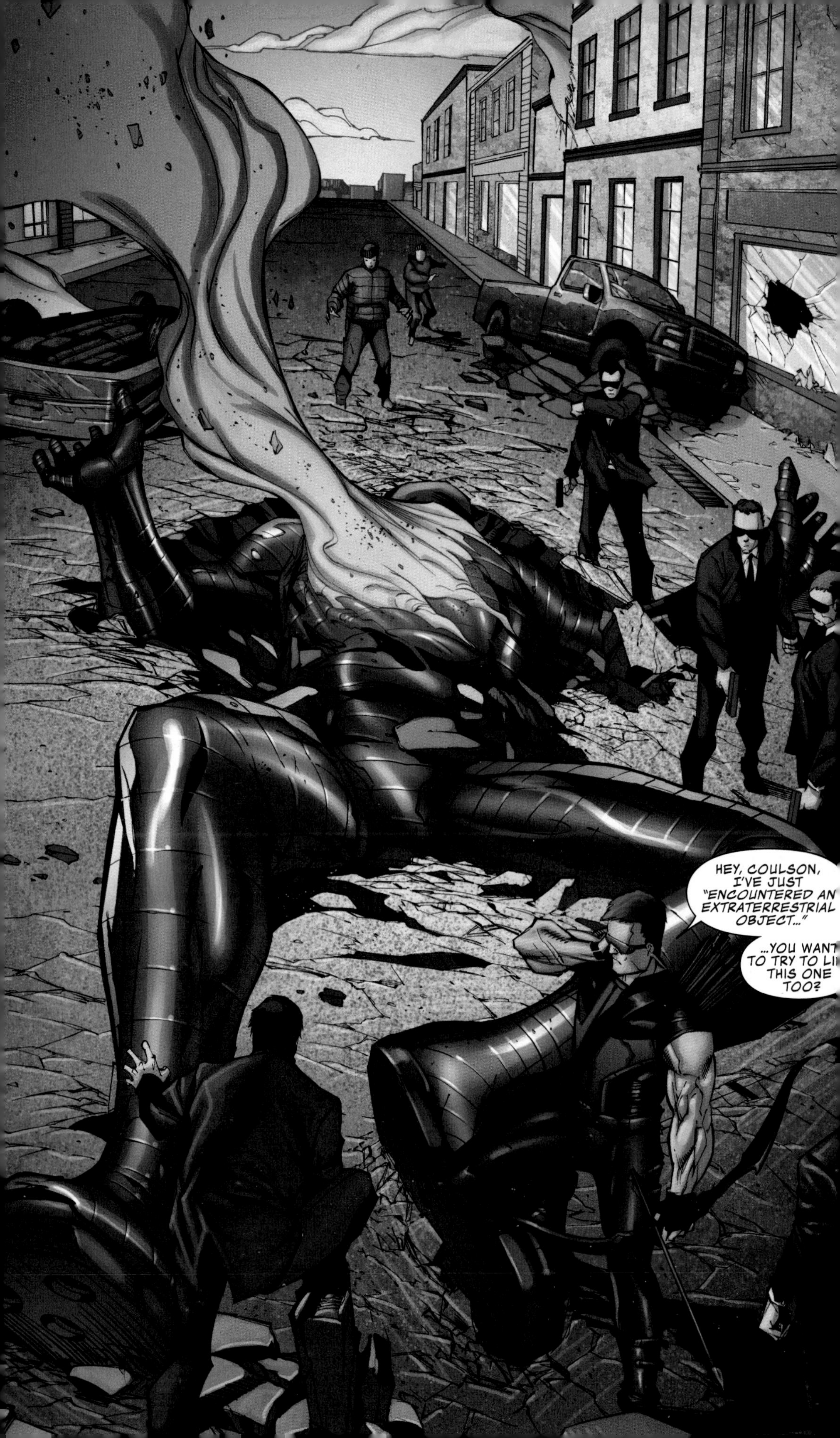
HEY, COULSON, I'VE JUST "ENCOUNTERED AN EXTRATERRESTRIAL OBJECT..."
...YOU WANT TO TRY TO LI THIS ONE TOO?

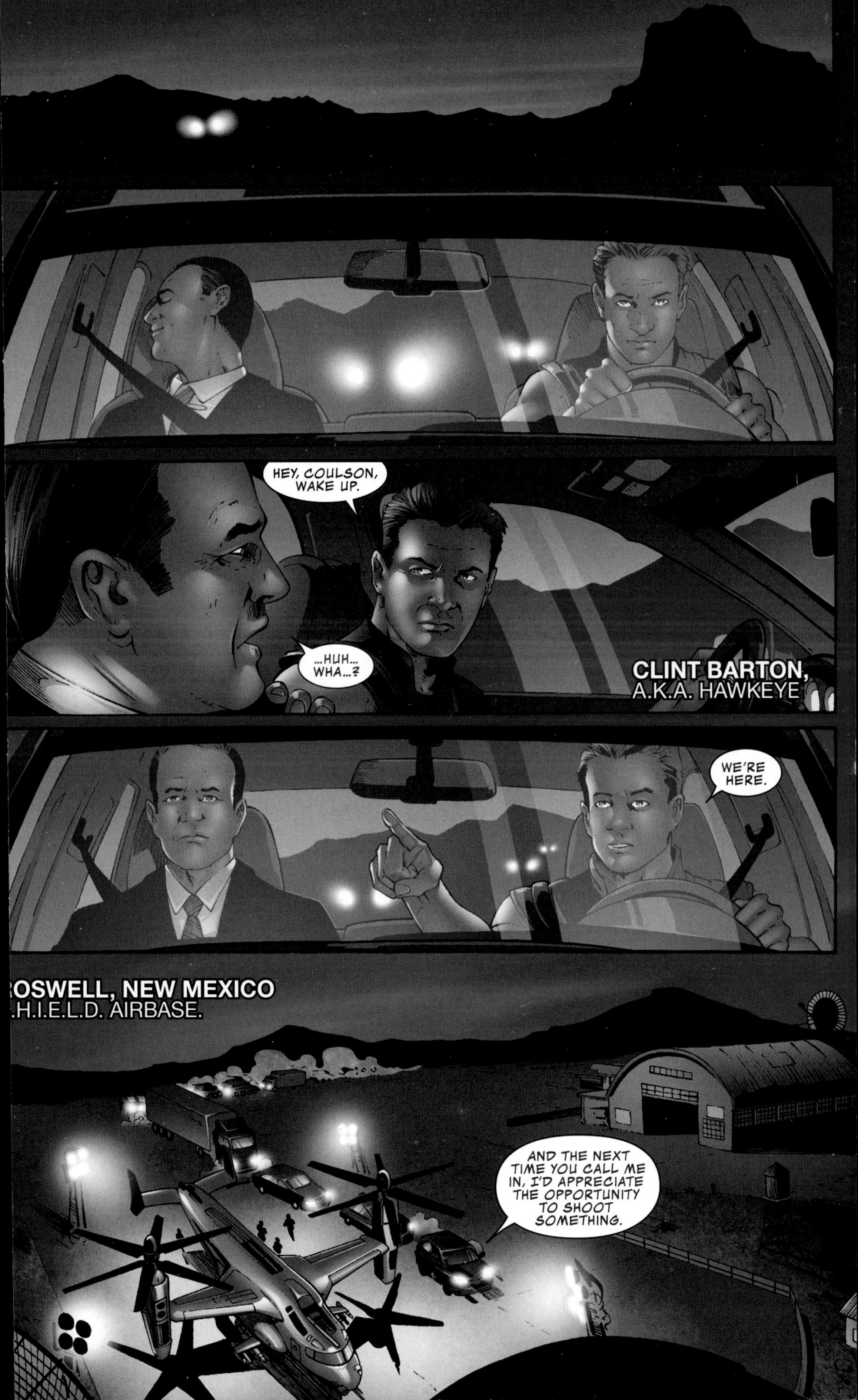
HEY, COULSON, WAKE UP.
...HUH... WHA...?
CLINT BARTON, A.K.A. HAWKEYE
WE'RE HERE.
ROSWELL, NEW MEXICO
.H.I.E.L.D. AIRBASE.
AND THE NEXT TIME YOU CALL ME IN, I'D APPRECIATE THE OPPORTUNITY TO SHOOT SOMETHING.

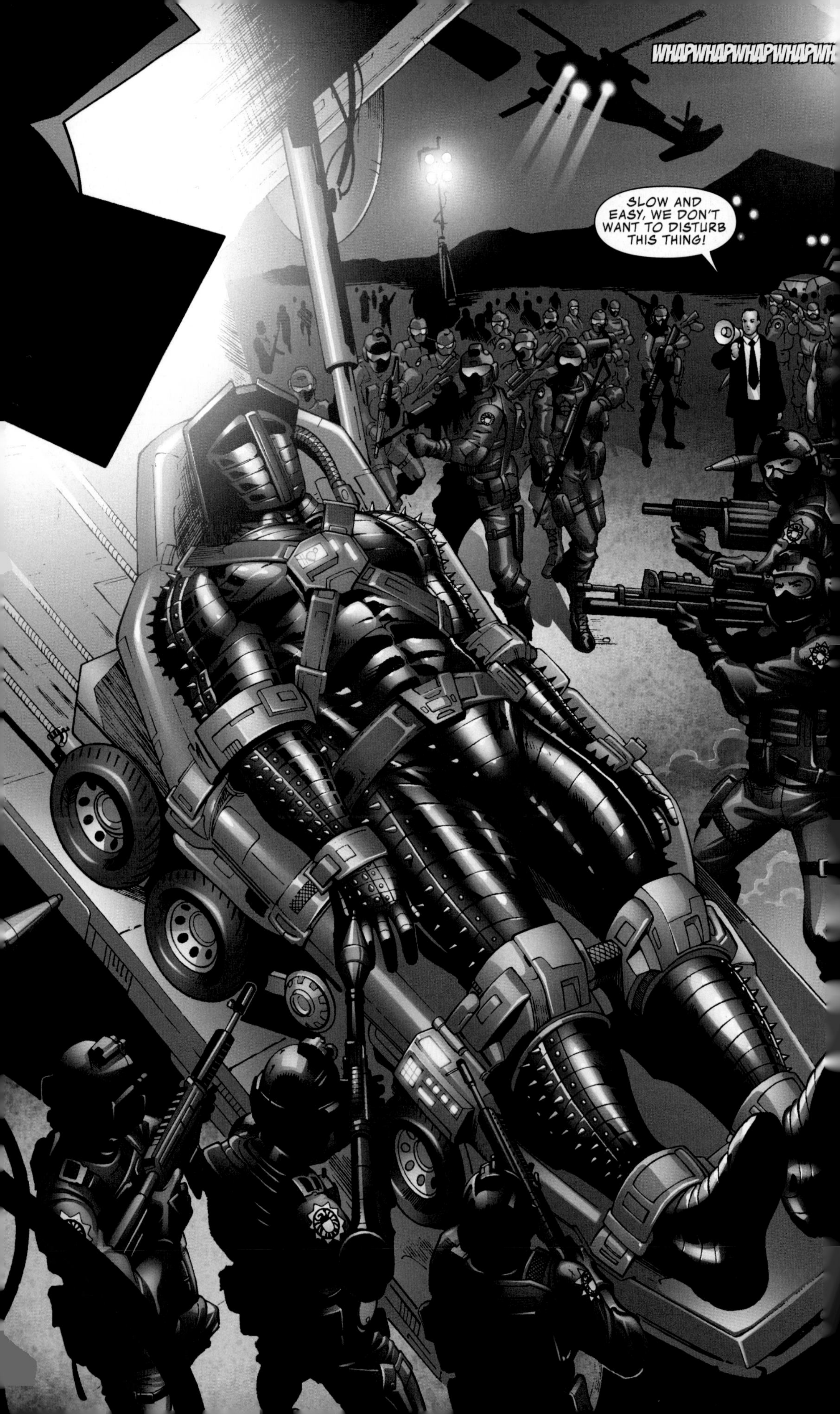
WHAPWHAPWHAPWHAPWH
SLOW AND EASY, WE DON'T WANT TO DISTURB THIS THING!

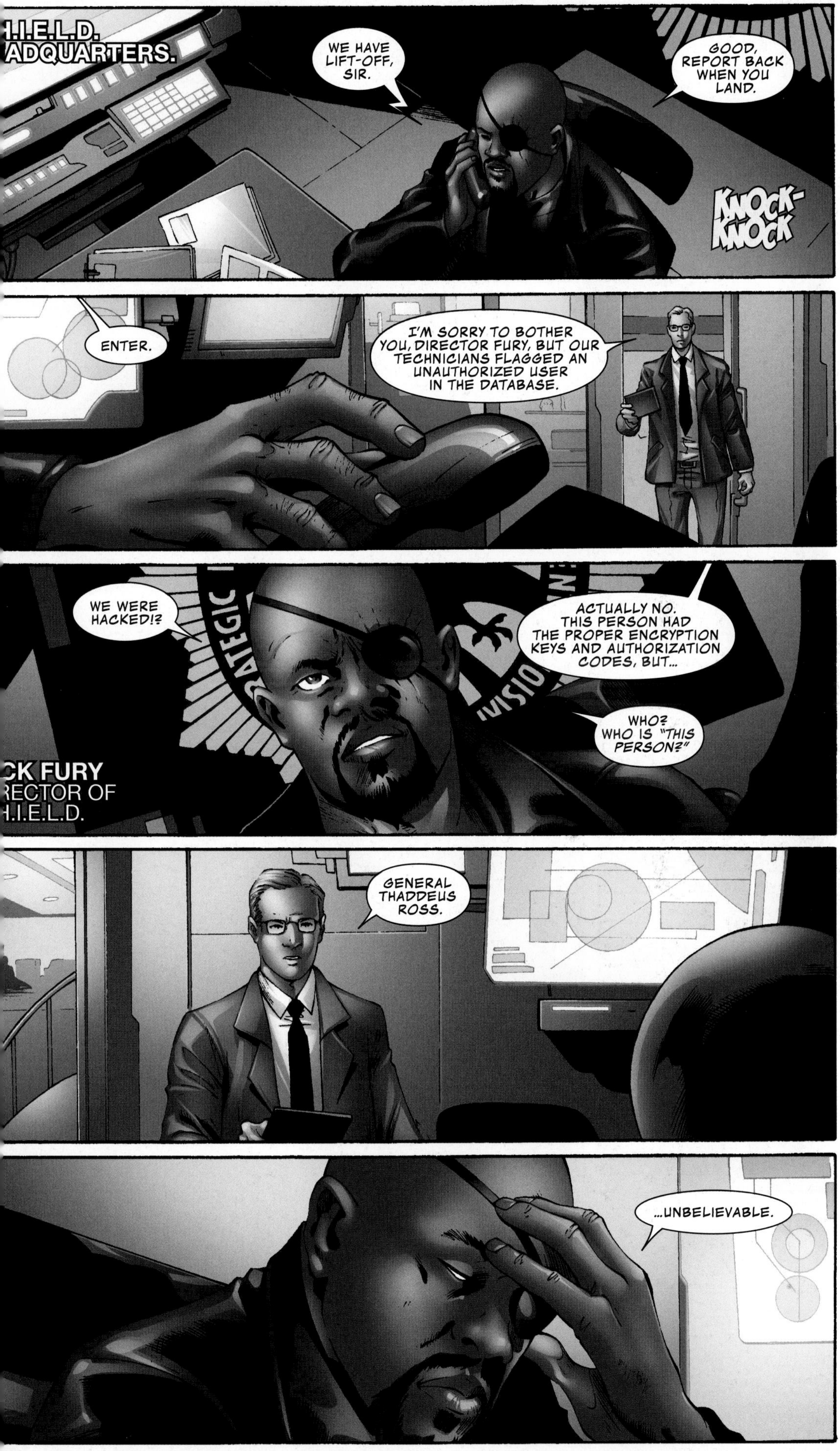

H.I.E.L.D.
ADQUARTERS.
WE HAVE LIFT-OFF, SIR.
GOOD, REPORT BACK WHEN YOU LAND.
KNOCK-KNOCK
ENTER.
I'M SORRY TO BOTHER YOU, DIRECTOR FURY, BUT OUR TECHNICIANS FLAGGED AN UNAUTHORIZED USER IN THE DATABASE.
WE WERE HACKED!?
ACTUALLY NO. THIS PERSON HAD THE PROPER ENCRYPTION KEYS AND AUTHORIZATION CODES, BUT...
WHO? WHO IS "THIS PERSON?"
CK FURY
RECTOR OF
H.I.E.L.D.
GENERAL THADDEUS ROSS.
...UNBELIEVABLE.

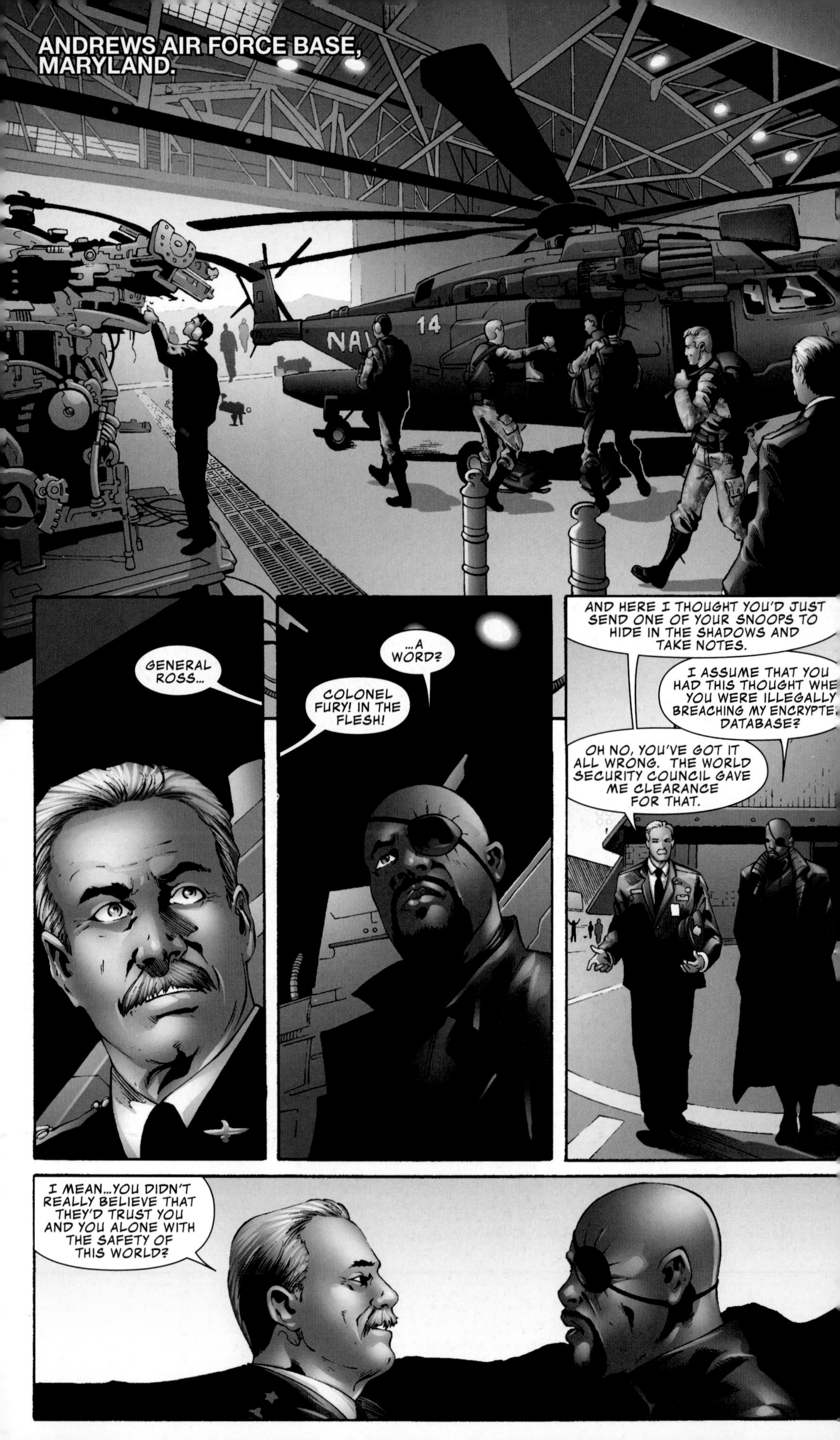
ANDREWS AIR FORCE BASE, MARYLAND.
14
GENERAL ROSS...
COLONEL FURY! IN THE FLESH!
...A WORD?
AND HERE I THOUGHT YOU'D JUST SEND ONE OF YOUR SNOOPS TO HIDE IN THE SHADOWS AND TAKE NOTES.
I ASSUME THAT YOU HAD THIS THOUGHT WHE YOU WERE ILLEGALLY BREACHING MY ENCRYPTE DATABASE?
OH NO, YOU'VE GOT IT ALL WRONG. THE WORLD SECURITY COUNCIL GAVE ME CLEARANCE FOR THAT.
I MEAN...YOU DIDN'T REALLY BELIEVE THAT THEY'D TRUST YOU AND YOU ALONE WITH THE SAFETY OF THIS WORLD?

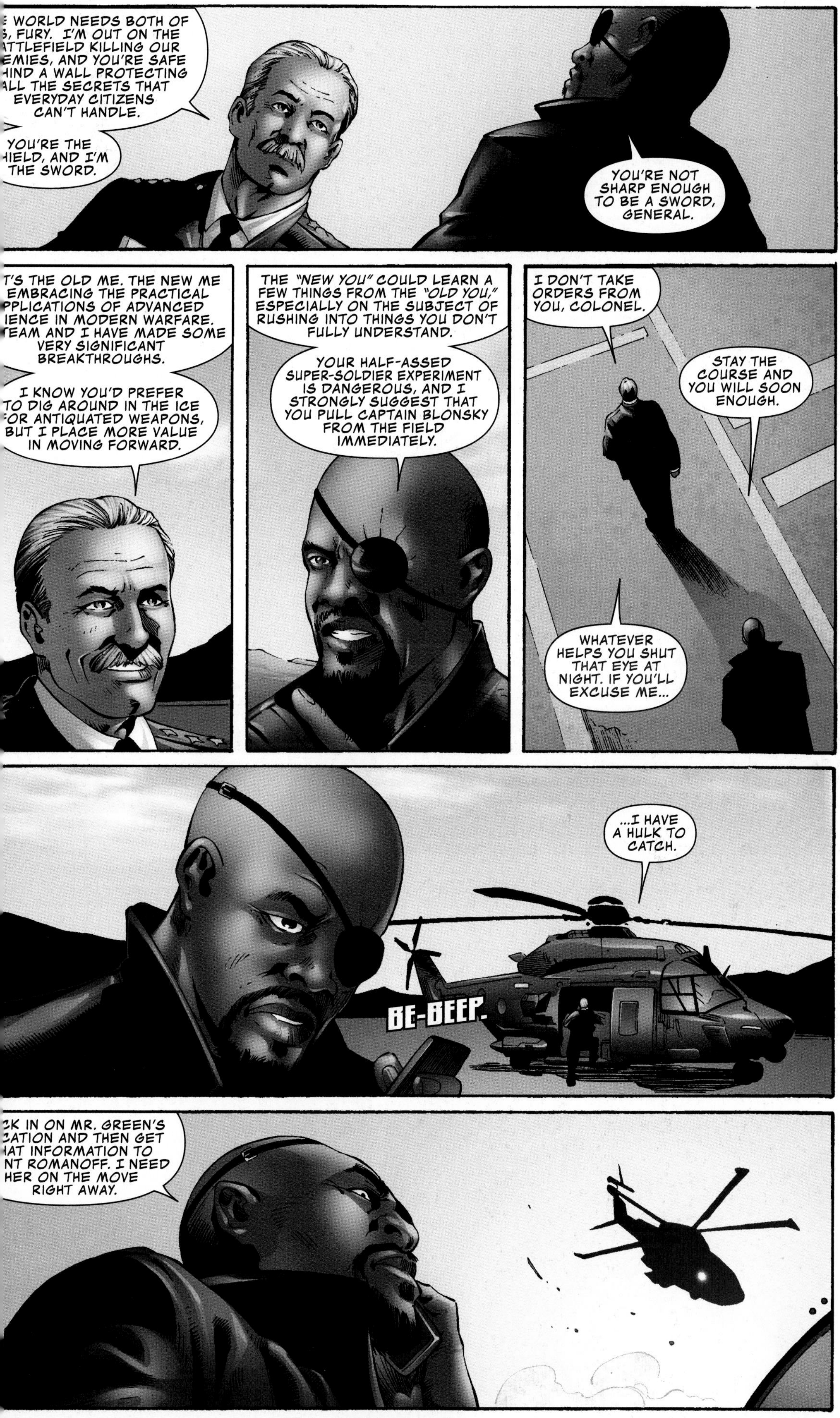
E WORLD NEEDS BOTH OF S, FURY. I'M OUT ON THE ATTLEFIELD KILLING OUR EMIES, AND YOU'RE SAFE HIND A WALL PROTECTING ALL THE SECRETS THAT EVERYDAY CITIZENS CAN'T HANDLE.
YOU'RE THE HIELD, AND I'M THE SWORD.
YOU'RE NOT SHARP ENOUGH TO BE A SWORD, GENERAL.
T'S THE OLD ME. THE NEW ME EMBRACING THE PRACTICAL PPLICATIONS OF ADVANCED IENCE IN MODERN WARFARE. TEAM AND I HAVE MADE SOME VERY SIGNIFICANT BREAKTHROUGHS.
I KNOW YOU'D PREFER TO DIG AROUND IN THE ICE FOR ANTIQUATED WEAPONS, BUT I PLACE MORE VALUE IN MOVING FORWARD.
THE "NEW YOU" COULD LEARN A FEW THINGS FROM THE "OLD YOU," ESPECIALLY ON THE SUBJECT OF RUSHING INTO THINGS YOU DON'T FULLY UNDERSTAND.
YOUR HALF-ASSED SUPER-SOLDIER EXPERIMENT IS DANGEROUS, AND I STRONGLY SUGGEST THAT YOU PULL CAPTAIN BLONSKY FROM THE FIELD IMMEDIATELY.
I DON'T TAKE ORDERS FROM YOU, COLONEL.
STAY THE COURSE AND YOU WILL SOON ENOUGH.
WHATEVER HELPS YOU SHUT THAT EYE AT NIGHT. IF YOU'LL EXCUSE ME...
...I HAVE A HULK TO CATCH.
BE-BEEP.
CK IN ON MR. GREEN'S CATION AND THEN GET HAT INFORMATION TO NT ROMANOFF. I NEED HER ON THE MOVE RIGHT AWAY.

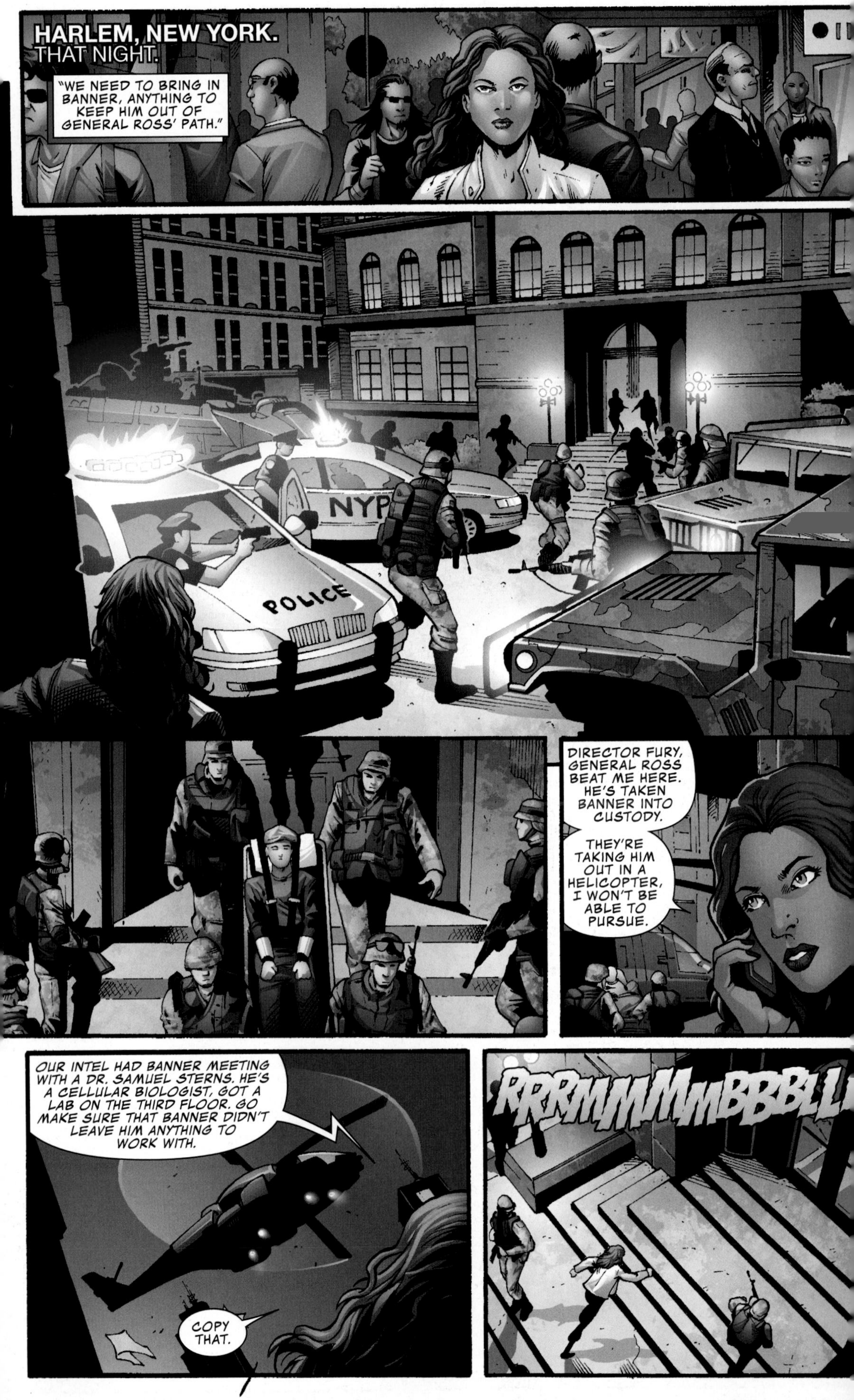
HARLEM, NEW YORK.
THAT NIGHT.
"WE NEED TO BRING IN BANNER, ANYTHING TO KEEP HIM OUT OF GENERAL ROSS' PATH."
NYP
POLICE
DIRECTOR FURY, GENERAL ROSS BEAT ME HERE. HE'S TAKEN BANNER INTO CUSTODY.
THEY'RE TAKING HIM OUT IN A HELICOPTER, I WON'T BE ABLE TO PURSUE.
OUR INTEL HAD BANNER MEETING WITH A DR. SAMUEL STERNS. HE'S A CELLULAR BIOLOGIST, GOT A LAB ON THE THIRD FLOOR. GO MAKE SURE THAT BANNER DIDN'T LEAVE HIM ANYTHING TO WORK WITH.
COPY THAT.
RRRMMMMMBBBLL

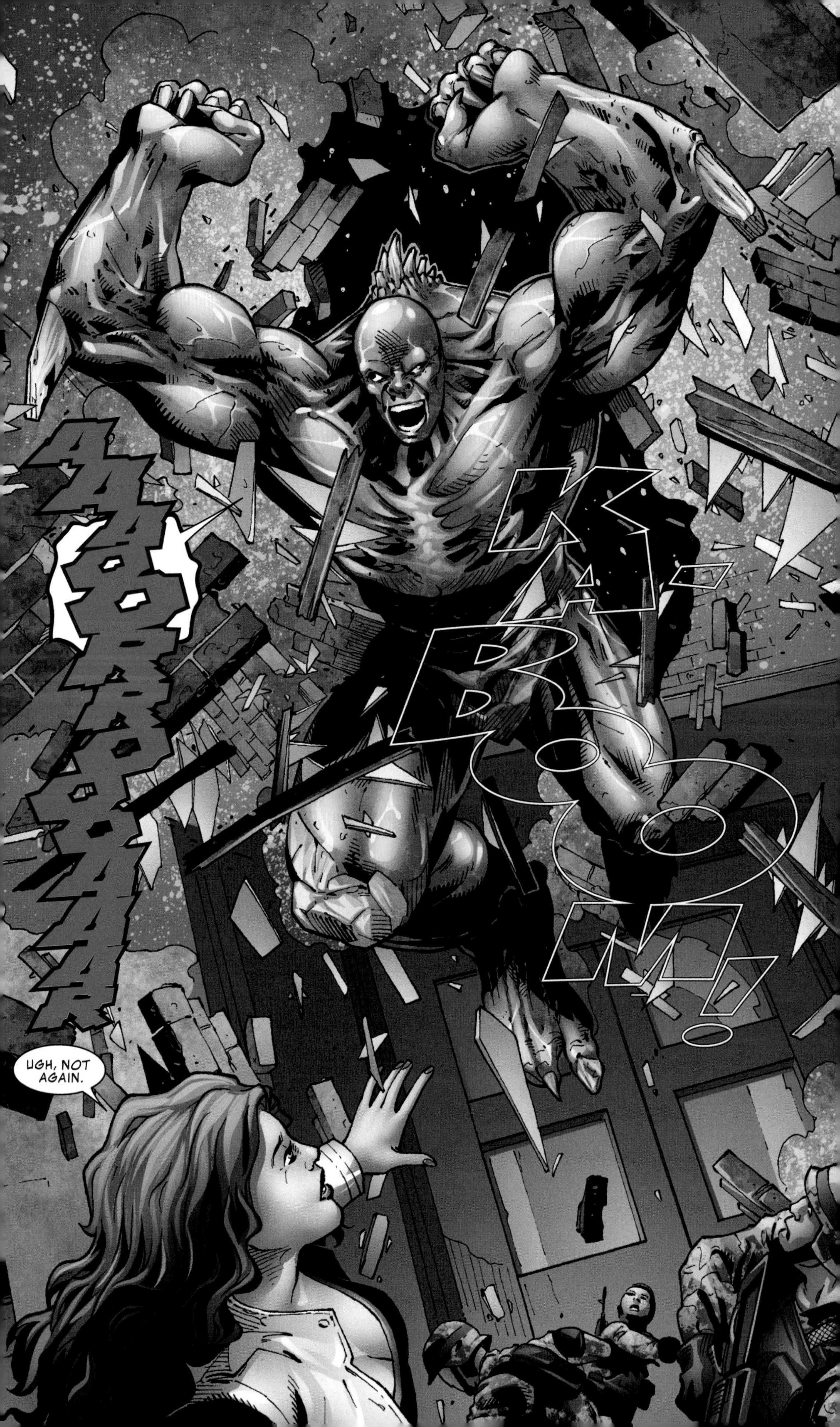
KA-BOOM!
UGH, NOT AGAIN.

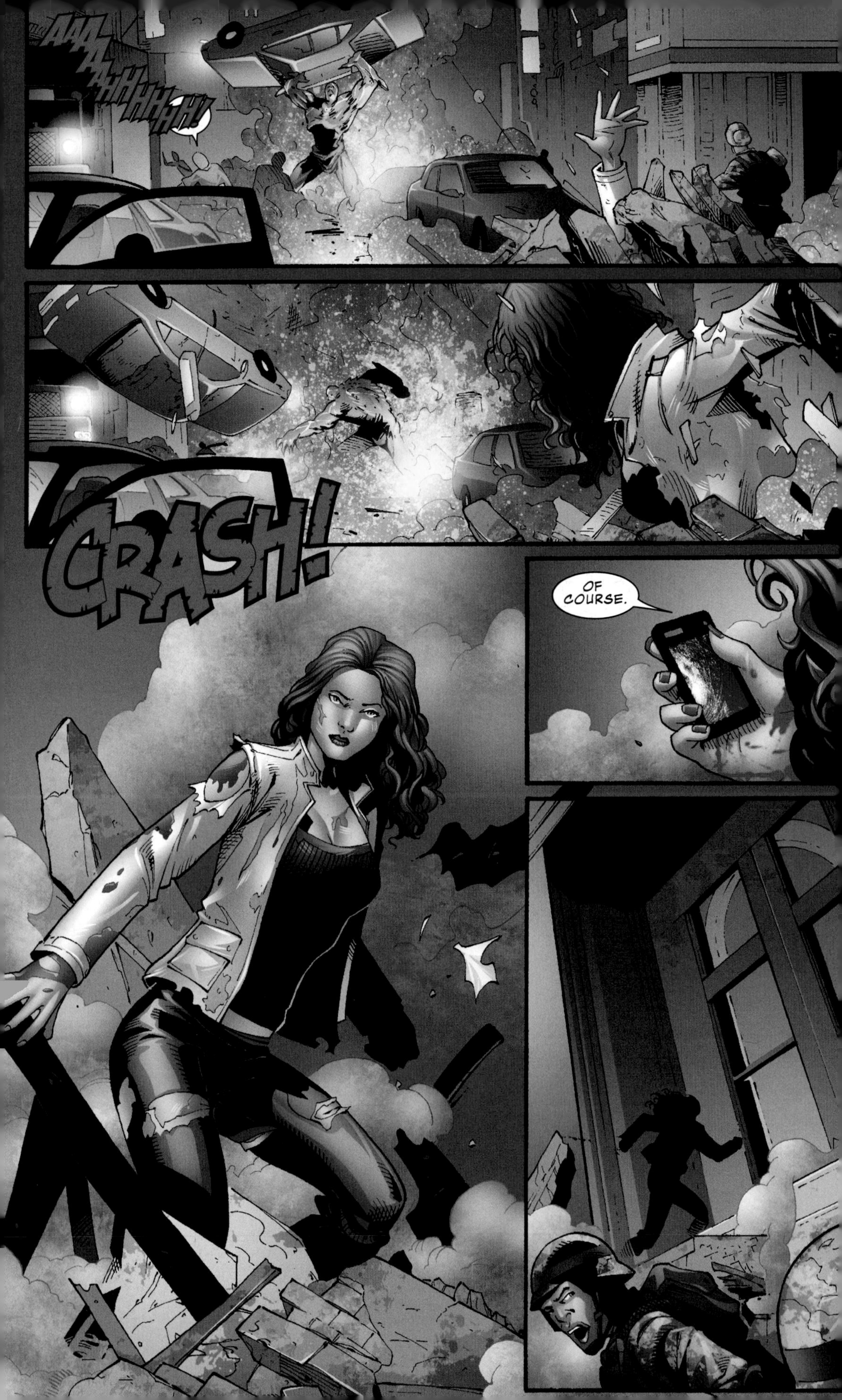
AAAAAHHHHHH!
CRASH!
OF COURSE.

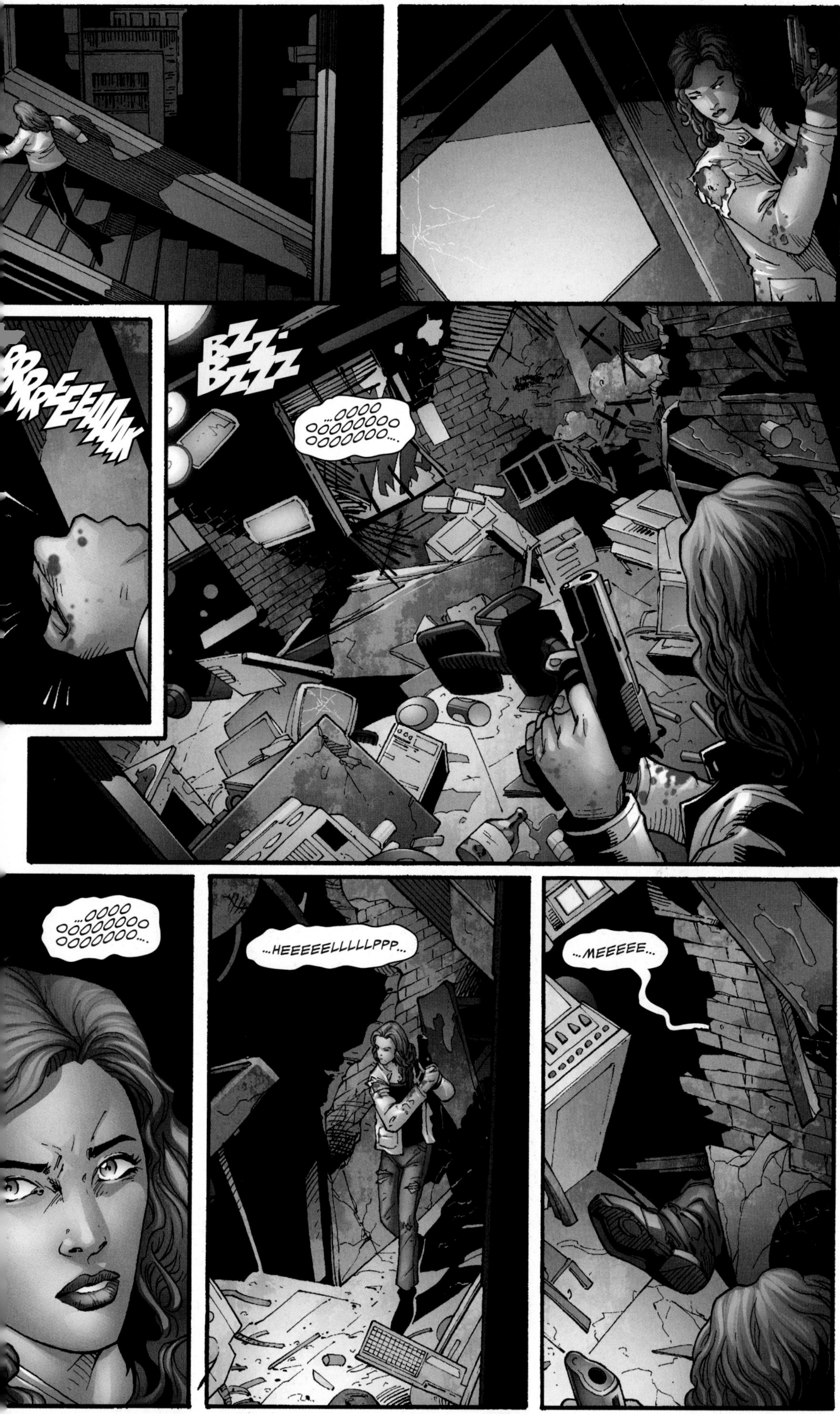

BZZ-BZZZ
...OOOO OOOOOOOO OOOOOOO....
...OOOO OOOOOOOO OOOOOOO....
...HEEEEELLLLLPPP...
...MEEEEE...

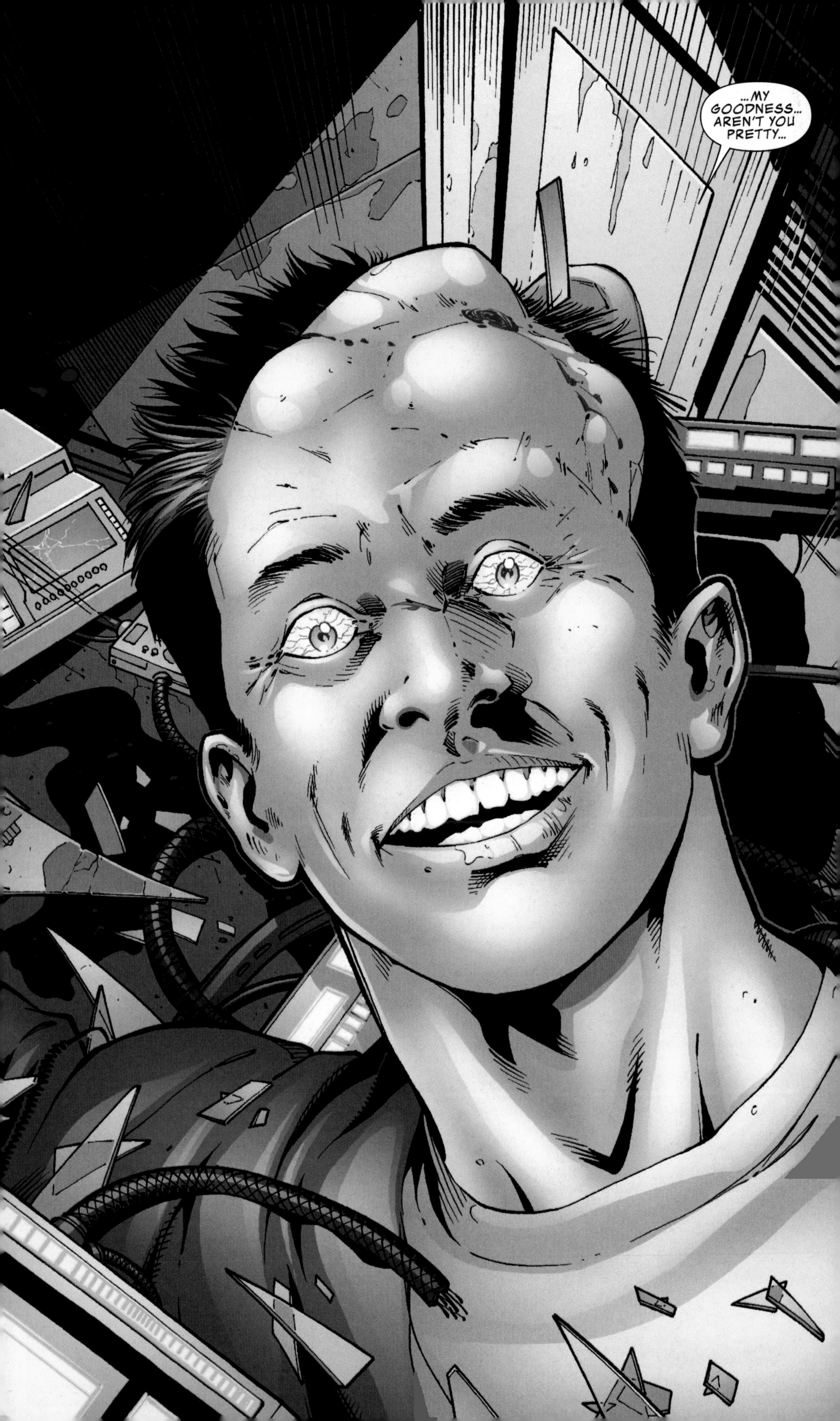
...MY GOODNESS... AREN'T YOU PRETTY...

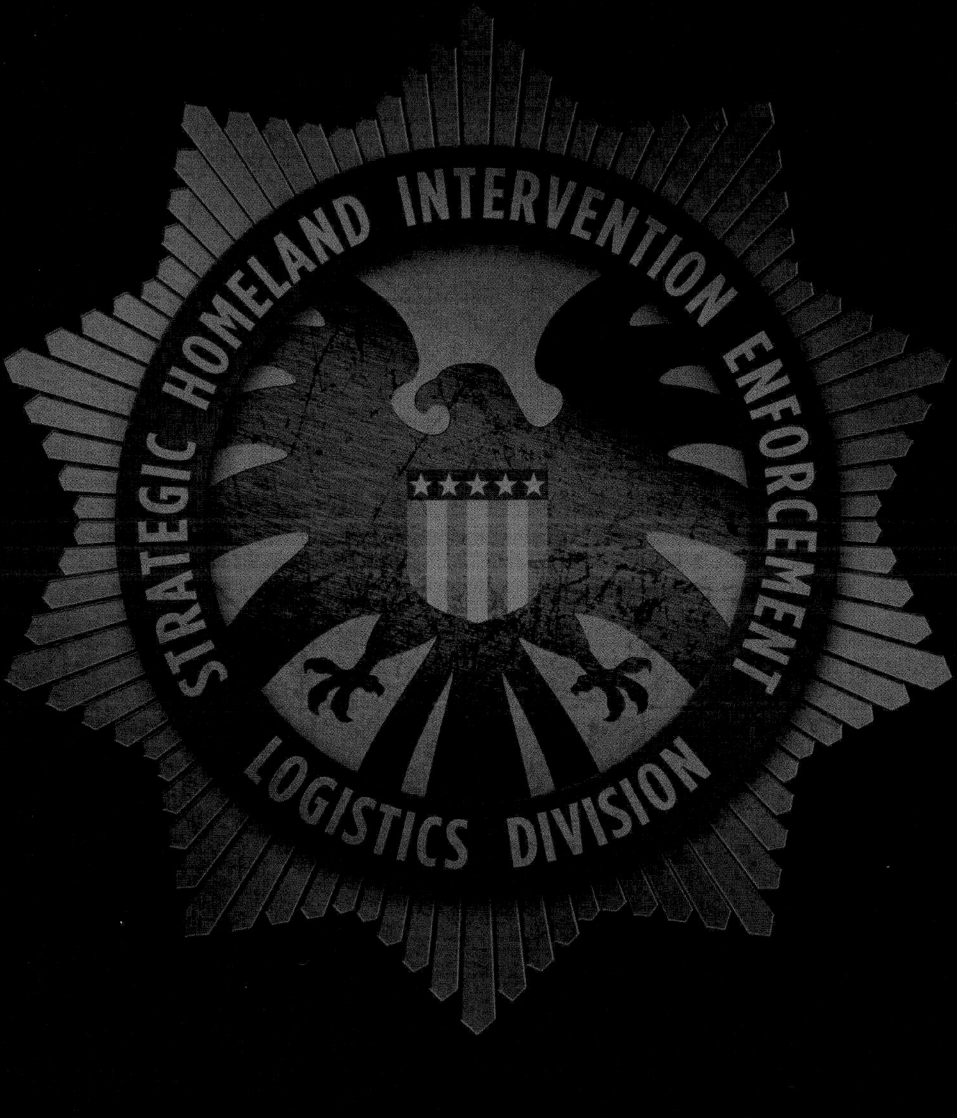
STRATEGIC HOMELAND INTERVENTION ENFORCEMENT
LOGISTICS DIVISION

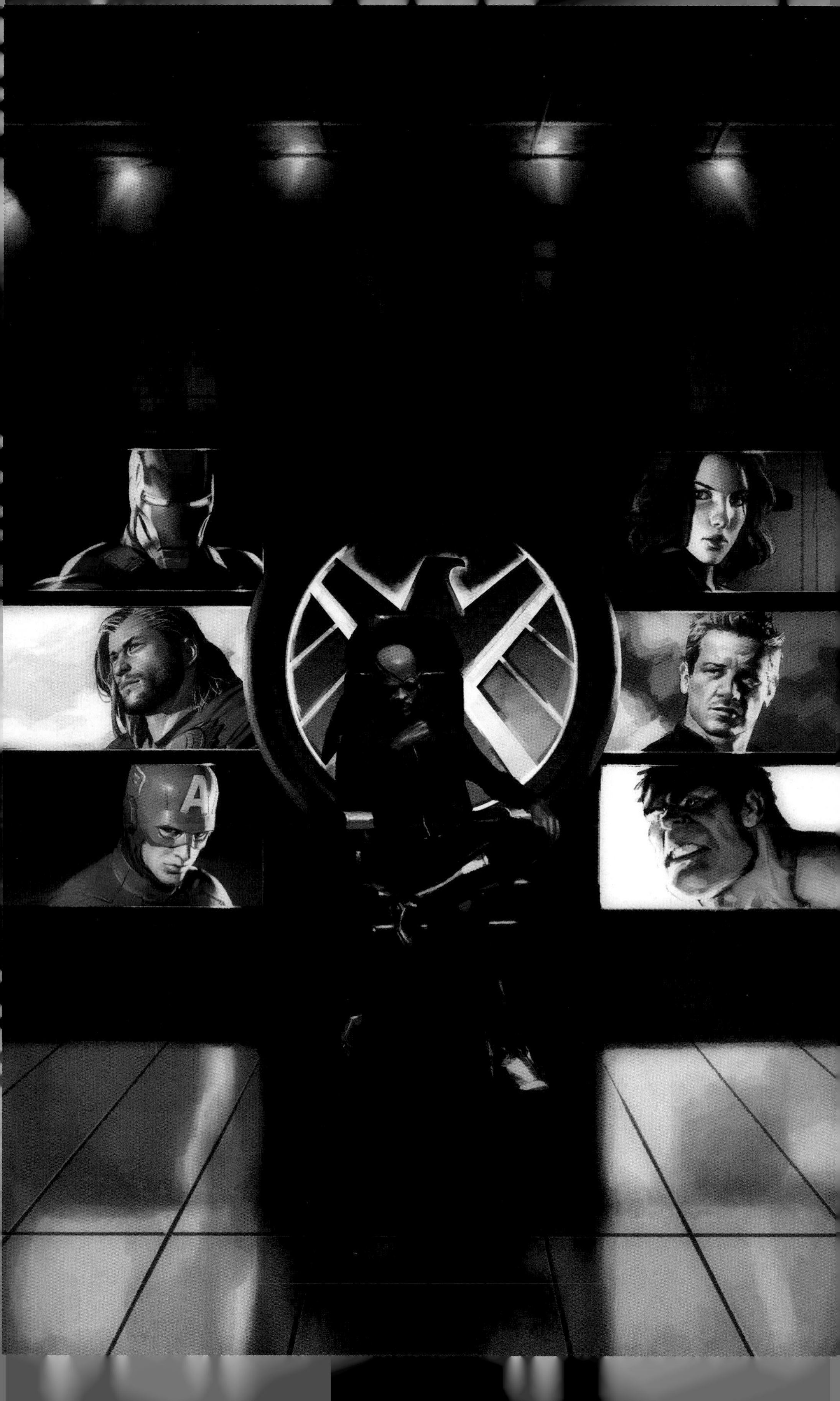

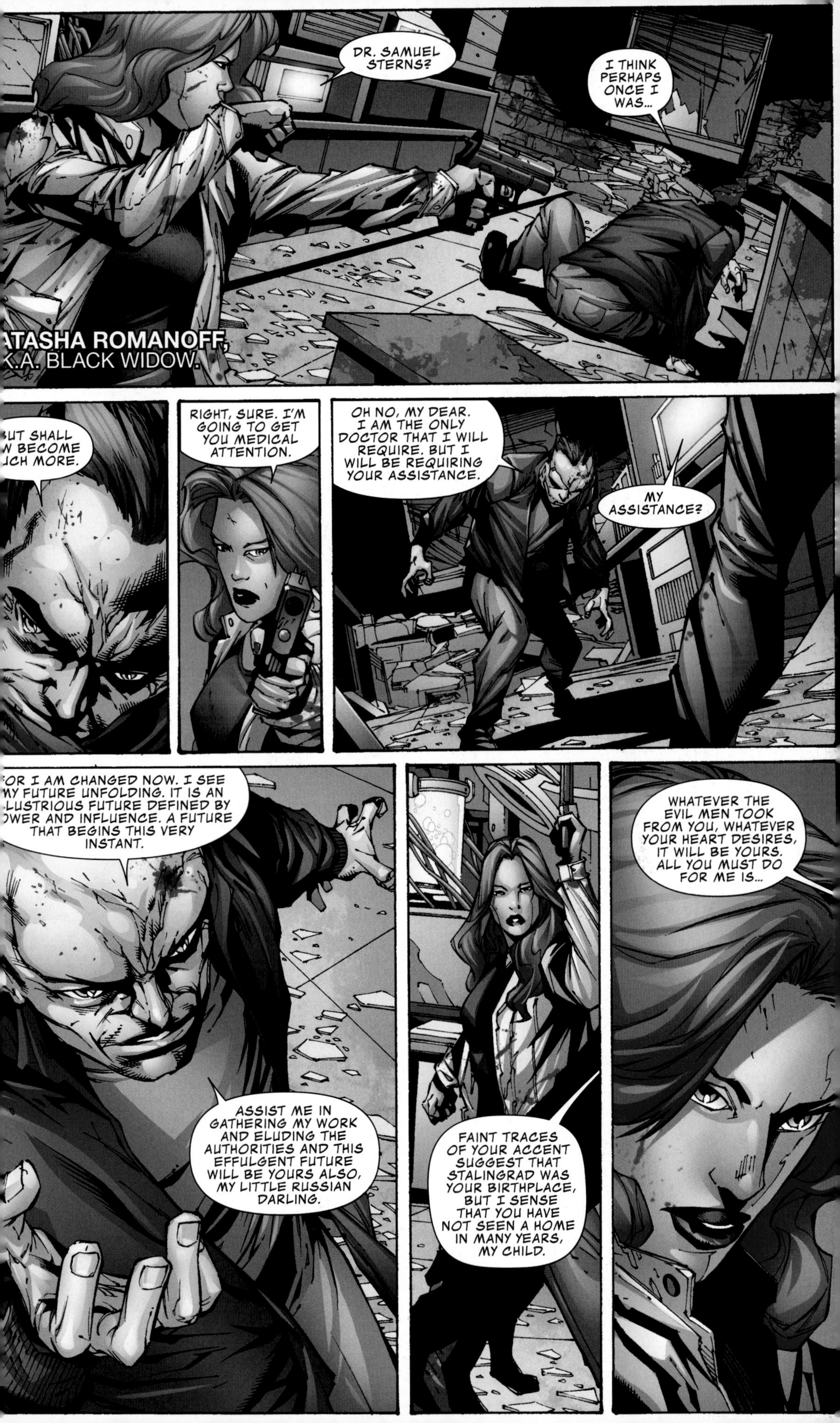
DR. SAMUEL STERNS?
I THINK PERHAPS ONCE I WAS...
ATASHA ROMANOFF, K.A. BLACK WIDOW.
UT SHALL W BECOME ICH MORE.
RIGHT, SURE. I'M GOING TO GET YOU MEDICAL ATTENTION.
OH NO, MY DEAR. I AM THE ONLY DOCTOR THAT I WILL REQUIRE. BUT I WILL BE REQUIRING YOUR ASSISTANCE.
MY ASSISTANCE?
FOR I AM CHANGED NOW. I SEE MY FUTURE UNFOLDING. IT IS AN LUSTRIOUS FUTURE DEFINED BY OWER AND INFLUENCE. A FUTURE THAT BEGINS THIS VERY INSTANT.
ASSIST ME IN GATHERING MY WORK AND ELUDING THE AUTHORITIES AND THIS EFFULGENT FUTURE WILL BE YOURS ALSO, MY LITTLE RUSSIAN DARLING.
FAINT TRACES OF YOUR ACCENT SUGGEST THAT STALINGRAD WAS YOUR BIRTHPLACE, BUT I SENSE THAT YOU HAVE NOT SEEN A HOME IN MANY YEARS, MY CHILD.
WHATEVER THE EVIL MEN TOOK FROM YOU, WHATEVER YOUR HEART DESIRES, IT WILL BE YOURS. ALL YOU MUST DO FOR ME IS...

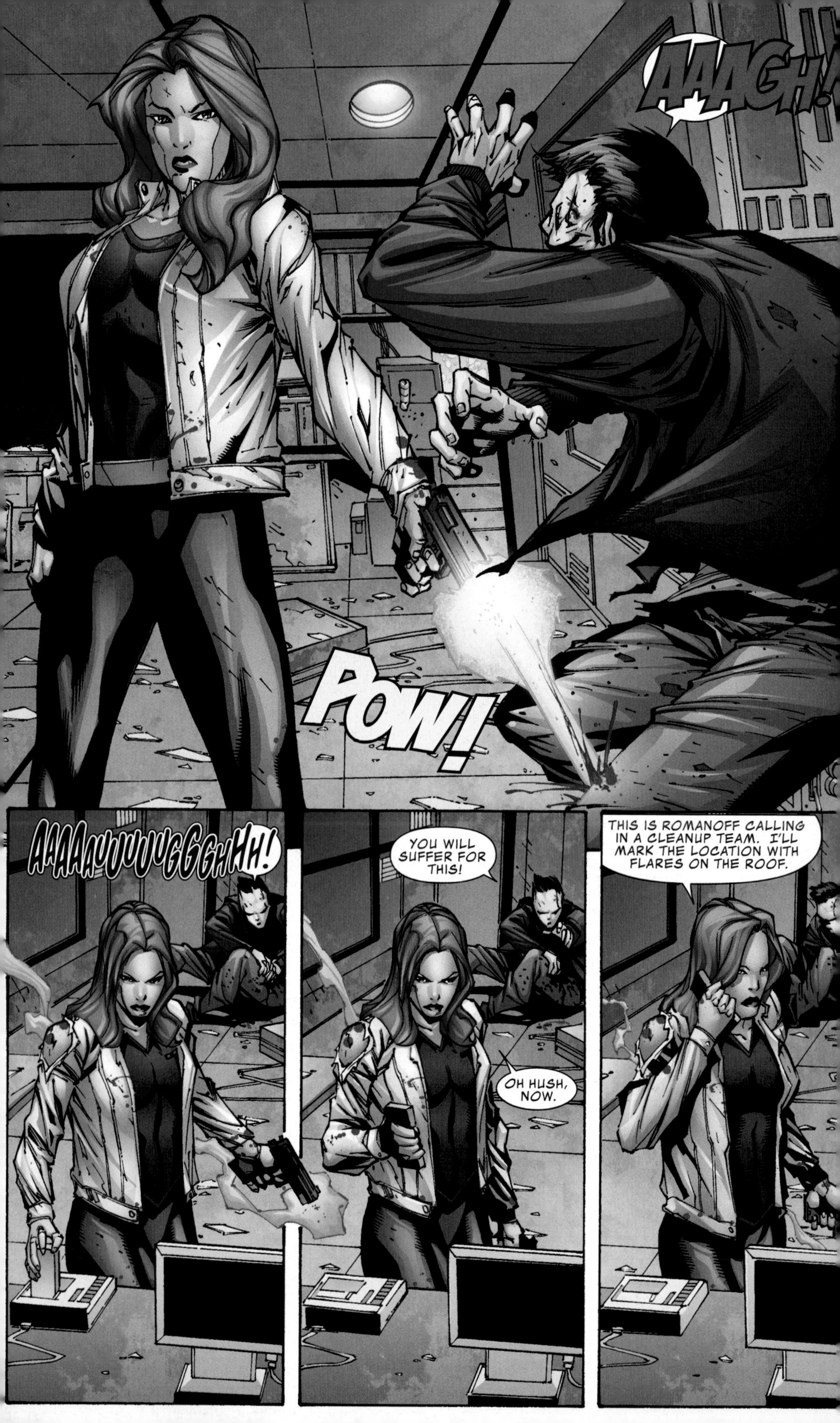
AAAGH!
POW!
AAAAAUUUUUGGGHHH!
YOU WILL SUFFER FOR THIS!
OH HUSH, NOW.
THIS IS ROMANOFF CALLING IN A CLEANUP TEAM. I'LL MARK THE LOCATION WITH FLARES ON THE ROOF.

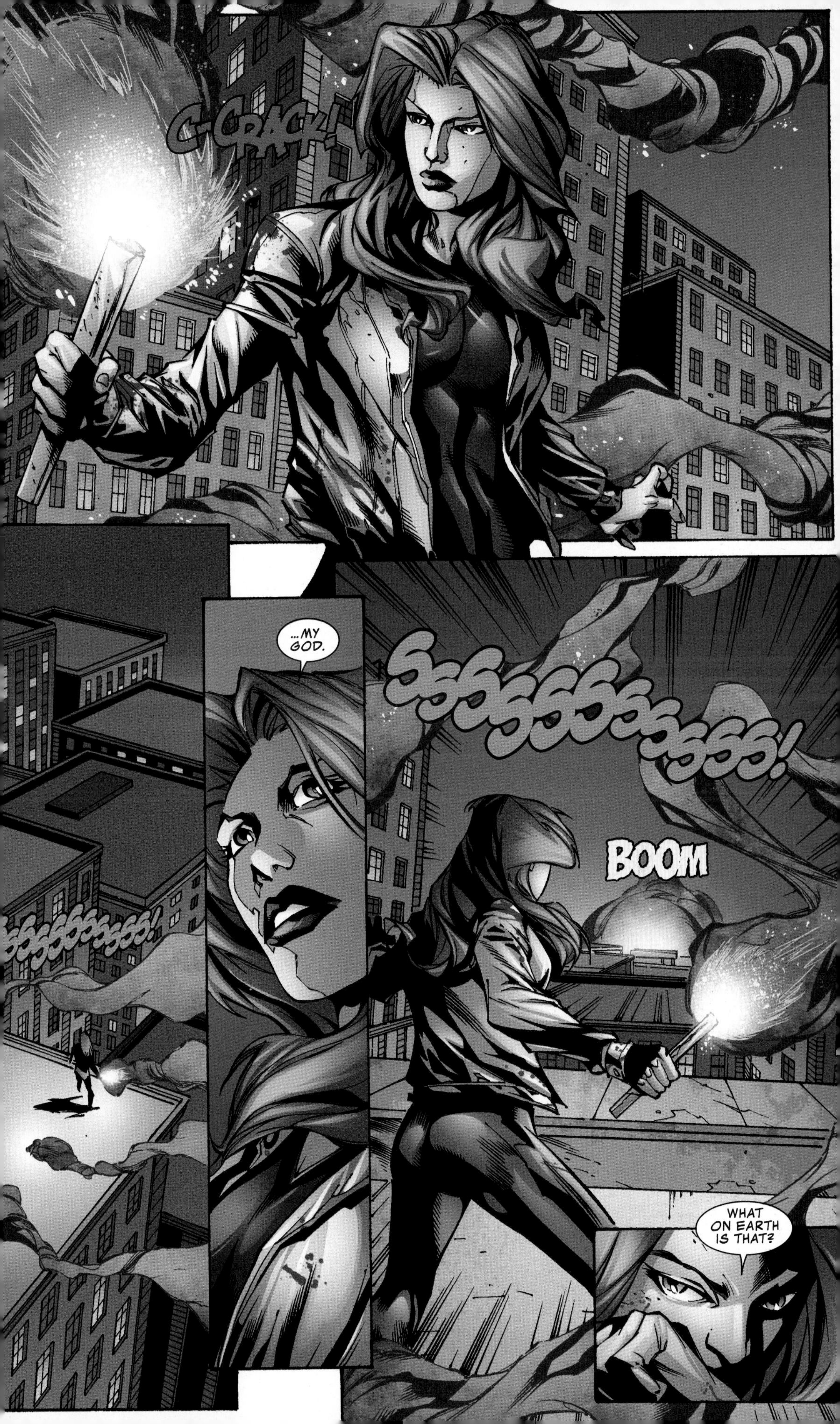
C-CRACK!
...MY GOD.
SSSSSSSSSSSSS!
SSSSSSSSSSSSS!
BOOM
WHAT ON EARTH IS THAT?

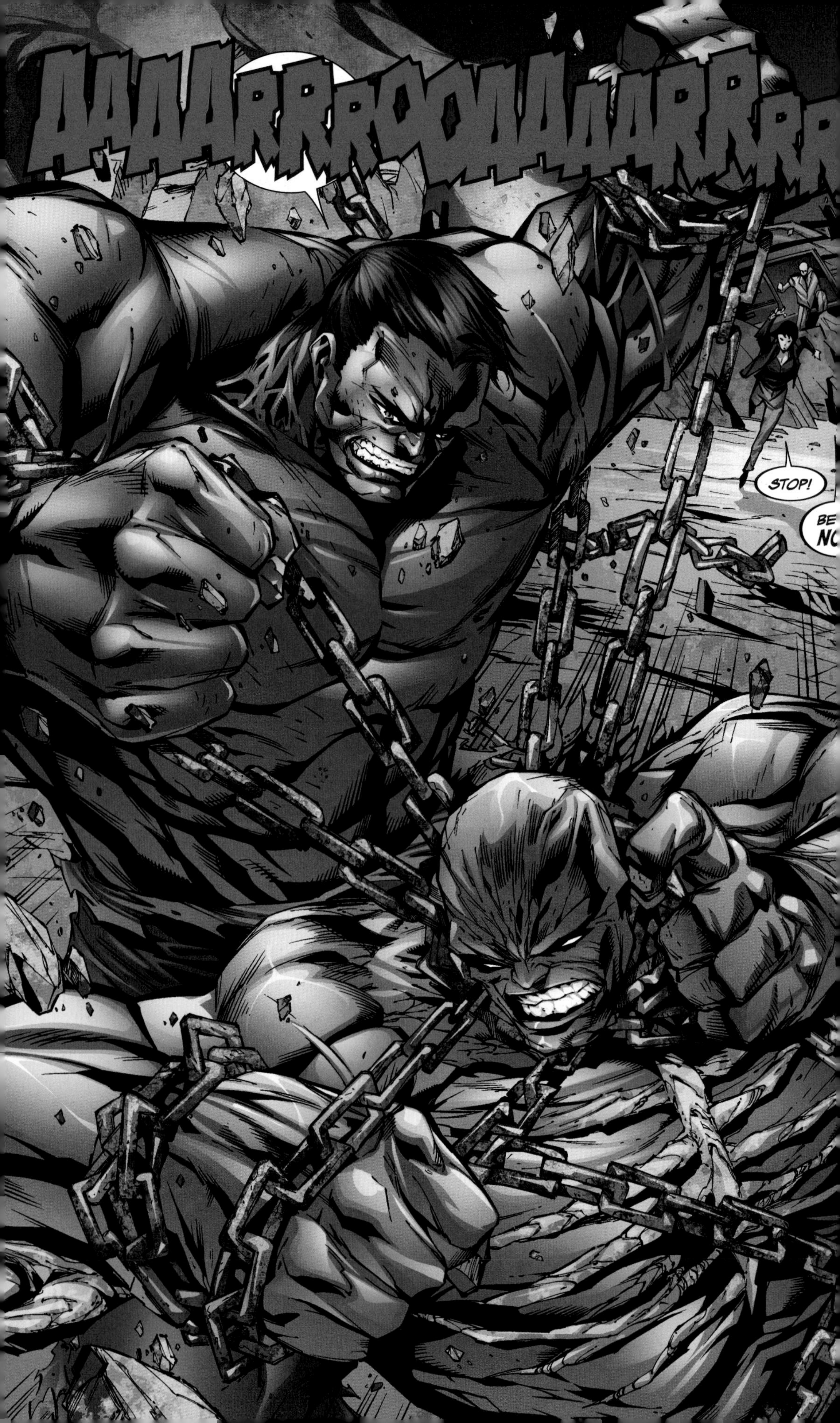
AAARRROAAAARRRR
STOP!
BE
NO

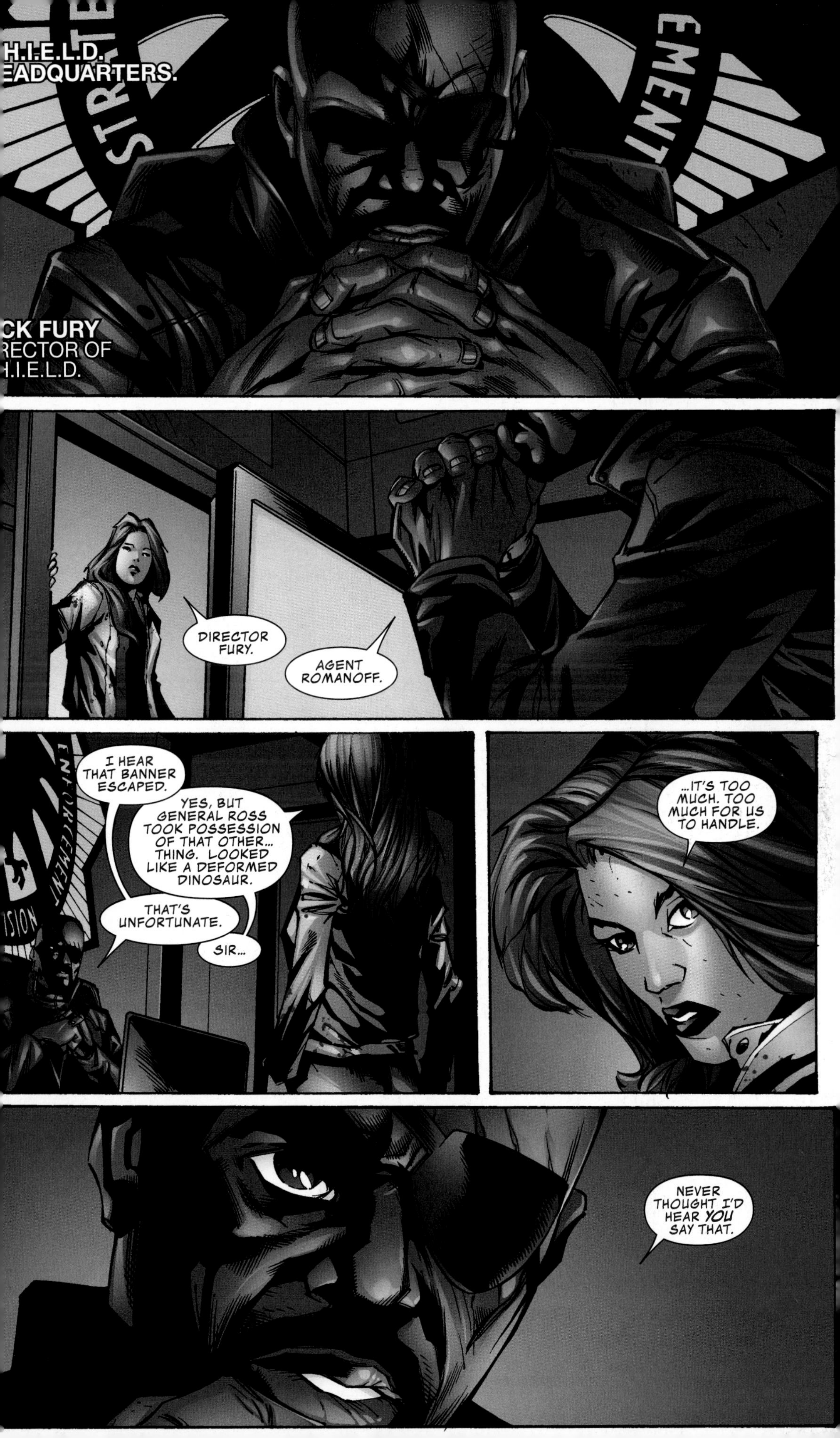

H.I.E.L.D.
EADQUARTERS.
CK FURY
RECTOR OF
H.I.E.L.D.
DIRECTOR FURY.
AGENT ROMANOFF.
I HEAR THAT BANNER ESCAPED.
YES, BUT GENERAL ROSS TOOK POSSESSION OF THAT OTHER... THING. LOOKED LIKE A DEFORMED DINOSAUR.
THAT'S UNFORTUNATE.
SIR...
...IT'S TOO MUCH. TOO MUCH FOR US TO HANDLE.
NEVER THOUGHT I'D HEAR *YOU* SAY THAT.

DON'T MISUNDERSTAND ME BECAUSE I FEAR NO MAN... BUT THIS IS DIFFERENT. THESE ARE GODS AND MONSTERS AND MACHINES OF WAR THAT WE'RE MIXED UP WITH.

I'M SUPPOSED TO GO UP AGAINST THE HULK WITH 17 ROUNDS OF ARMOR-PIERCING BULLETS? I DON'T THINK SO.

I DON'T LIKE IT ANY MORE THAN YOU DO, SIR... BUT WE ARE OUTMATCHED. THE SOONER WE ACCEPT IT THE SOONER WE CAN FIX IT... OR THE SOONER WE CAN STOP WASTING OUR TIME PRETENDING THAT WE CAN MAKE A DIFFERENCE.

YOU'RE RIG AND I'D L YOU TO SE SOMETHIN

PLEASE HOLD FOR THE WORLD SECURITY COUNCIL...

PLEASE HOLD FOR THE WORLD SECURITY COUNCIL...

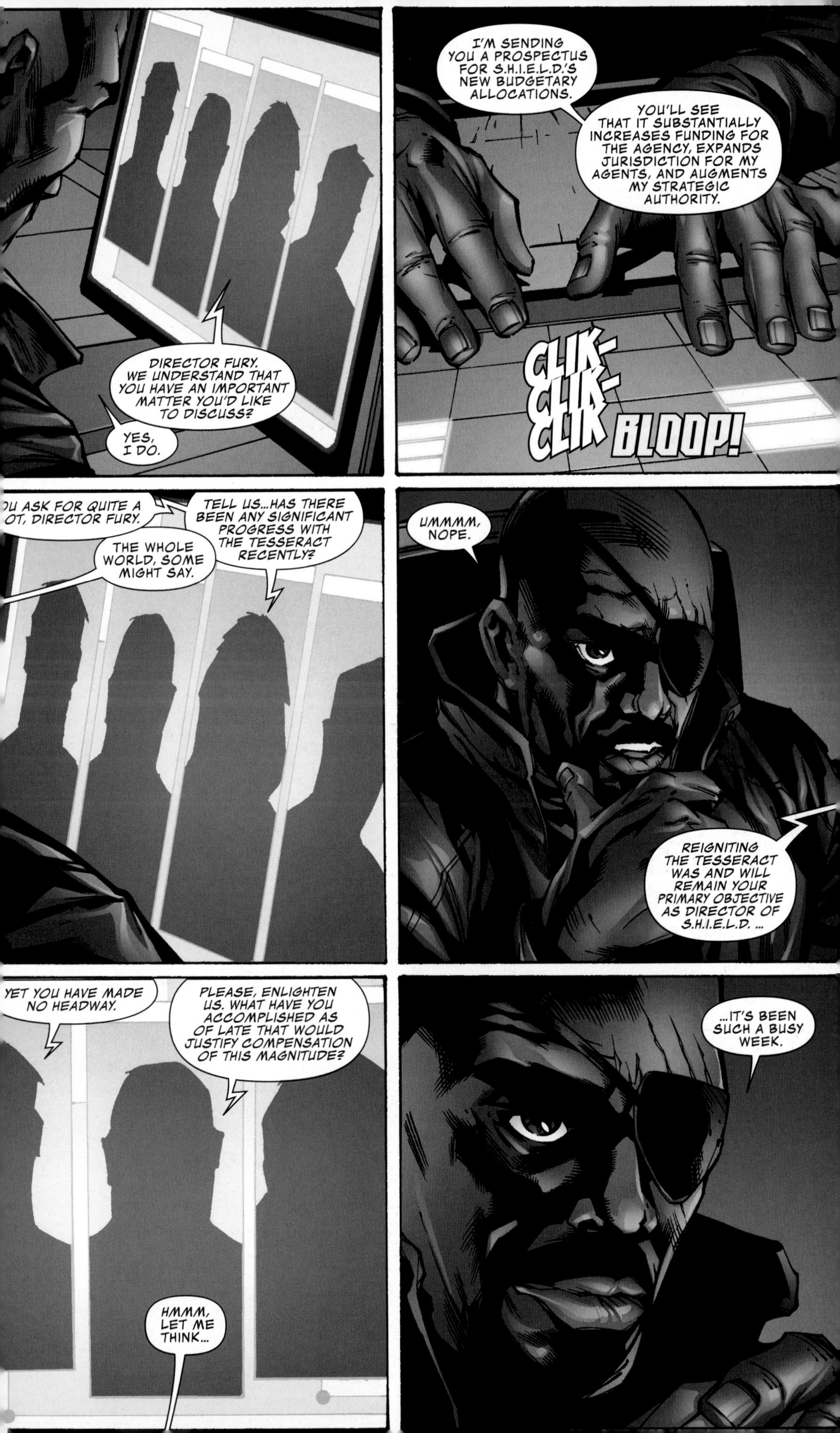
DIRECTOR FURY. WE UNDERSTAND THAT YOU HAVE AN IMPORTANT MATTER YOU'D LIKE TO DISCUSS?
YES, I DO.
I'M SENDING YOU A PROSPECTUS FOR S.H.I.E.L.D.'S NEW BUDGETARY ALLOCATIONS.
YOU'LL SEE THAT IT SUBSTANTIALLY INCREASES FUNDING FOR THE AGENCY, EXPANDS JURISDICTION FOR MY AGENTS, AND AUGMENTS MY STRATEGIC AUTHORITY.
CLIK-CLIK-CLIK
BLOOP!
OU ASK FOR QUITE A OT, DIRECTOR FURY.
THE WHOLE WORLD, SOME MIGHT SAY.
TELL US...HAS THERE BEEN ANY SIGNIFICANT PROGRESS WITH THE TESSERACT RECENTLY?
UMMMM, NOPE.
REIGNITING THE TESSERACT WAS AND WILL REMAIN YOUR PRIMARY OBJECTIVE AS DIRECTOR OF S.H.I.E.L.D. ...
YET YOU HAVE MADE NO HEADWAY.
PLEASE, ENLIGHTEN US. WHAT HAVE YOU ACCOMPLISHED AS OF LATE THAT WOULD JUSTIFY COMPENSATION OF THIS MAGNITUDE?
HMMM, LET ME THINK...
...IT'S BEEN SUCH A BUSY WEEK.

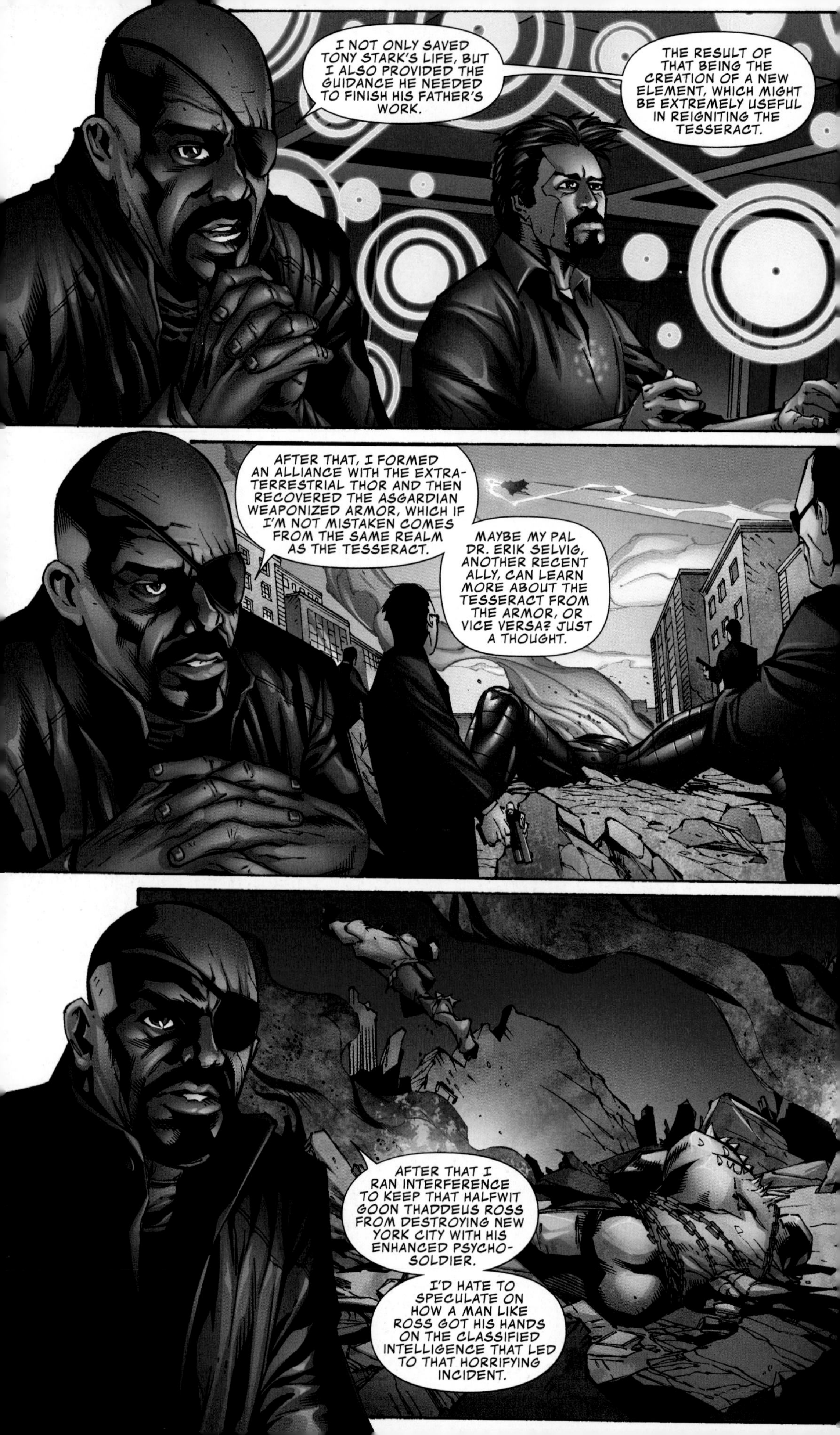
I NOT ONLY SAVED TONY STARK'S LIFE, BUT I ALSO PROVIDED THE GUIDANCE HE NEEDED TO FINISH HIS FATHER'S WORK.
THE RESULT OF THAT BEING THE CREATION OF A NEW ELEMENT, WHICH MIGHT BE EXTREMELY USEFUL IN REIGNITING THE TESSERACT.
AFTER THAT, I FORMED AN ALLIANCE WITH THE EXTRA-TERRESTRIAL THOR AND THEN RECOVERED THE ASGARDIAN WEAPONIZED ARMOR, WHICH IF I'M NOT MISTAKEN COMES FROM THE SAME REALM AS THE TESSERACT.
MAYBE MY PAL DR. ERIK SELVIG, ANOTHER RECENT ALLY, CAN LEARN MORE ABOUT THE TESSERACT FROM THE ARMOR, OR VICE VERSA? JUST A THOUGHT.
AFTER THAT I RAN INTERFERENCE TO KEEP THAT HALFWIT GOON THADDEUS ROSS FROM DESTROYING NEW YORK CITY WITH HIS ENHANCED PSYCHO-SOLDIER.
I'D HATE TO SPECULATE ON HOW A MAN LIKE ROSS GOT HIS HANDS ON THE CLASSIFIED INTELLIGENCE THAT LED TO THAT HORRIFYING INCIDENT.

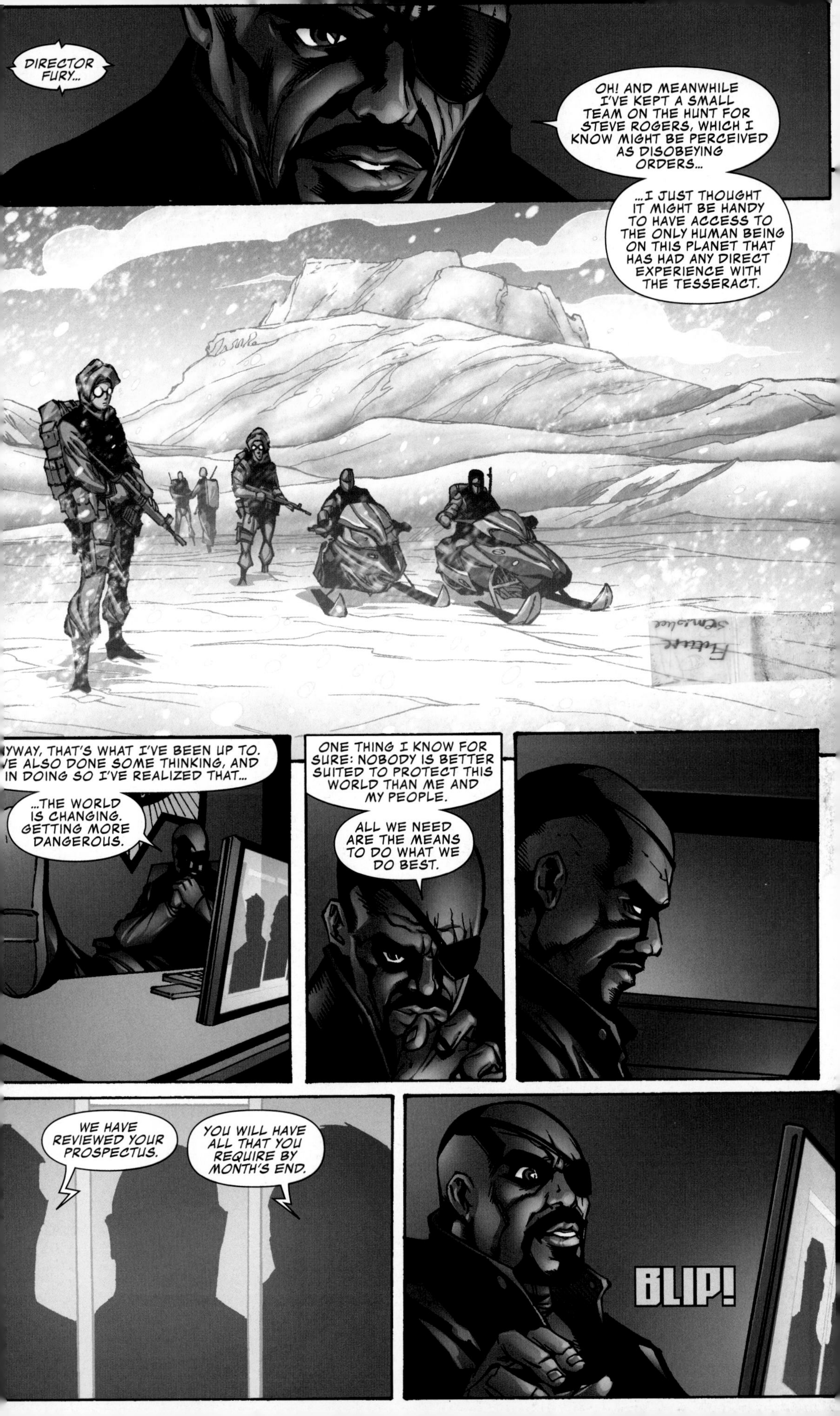
DIRECTOR FURY...
OH! AND MEANWHILE I'VE KEPT A SMALL TEAM ON THE HUNT FOR STEVE ROGERS, WHICH I KNOW MIGHT BE PERCEIVED AS DISOBEYING ORDERS...
...I JUST THOUGHT IT MIGHT BE HANDY TO HAVE ACCESS TO THE ONLY HUMAN BEING ON THIS PLANET THAT HAS HAD ANY DIRECT EXPERIENCE WITH THE TESSERACT.
YWAY, THAT'S WHAT I'VE BEEN UP TO. VE ALSO DONE SOME THINKING, AND IN DOING SO I'VE REALIZED THAT...
...THE WORLD IS CHANGING. GETTING MORE DANGEROUS.
ONE THING I KNOW FOR SURE: NOBODY IS BETTER SUITED TO PROTECT THIS WORLD THAN ME AND MY PEOPLE.
ALL WE NEED ARE THE MEANS TO DO WHAT WE DO BEST.
WE HAVE REVIEWED YOUR PROSPECTUS.
YOU WILL HAVE ALL THAT YOU REQUIRE BY MONTH'S END.
BLIP!

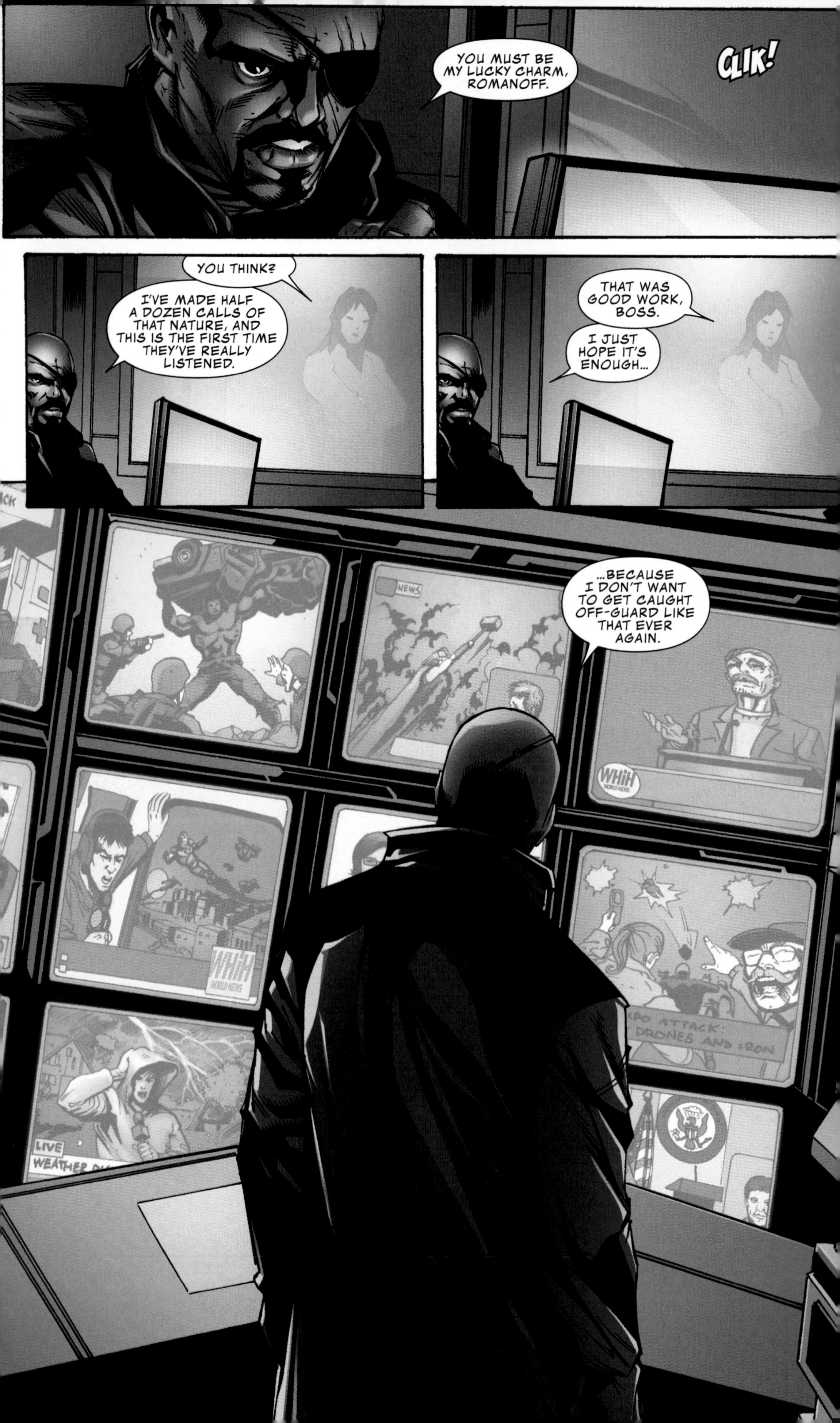
YOU MUST BE MY LUCKY CHARM, ROMANOFF.
CLIK!
YOU THINK?
I'VE MADE HALF A DOZEN CALLS OF THAT NATURE, AND THIS IS THE FIRST TIME THEY'VE REALLY LISTENED.
THAT WAS GOOD WORK, BOSS.
I JUST HOPE IT'S ENOUGH...
...BECAUSE I DON'T WANT TO GET CAUGHT OFF-GUARD LIKE THAT EVER AGAIN.
NEWS
WHiH WORLD NEWS
WHiH WORLD NEWS
LIVE

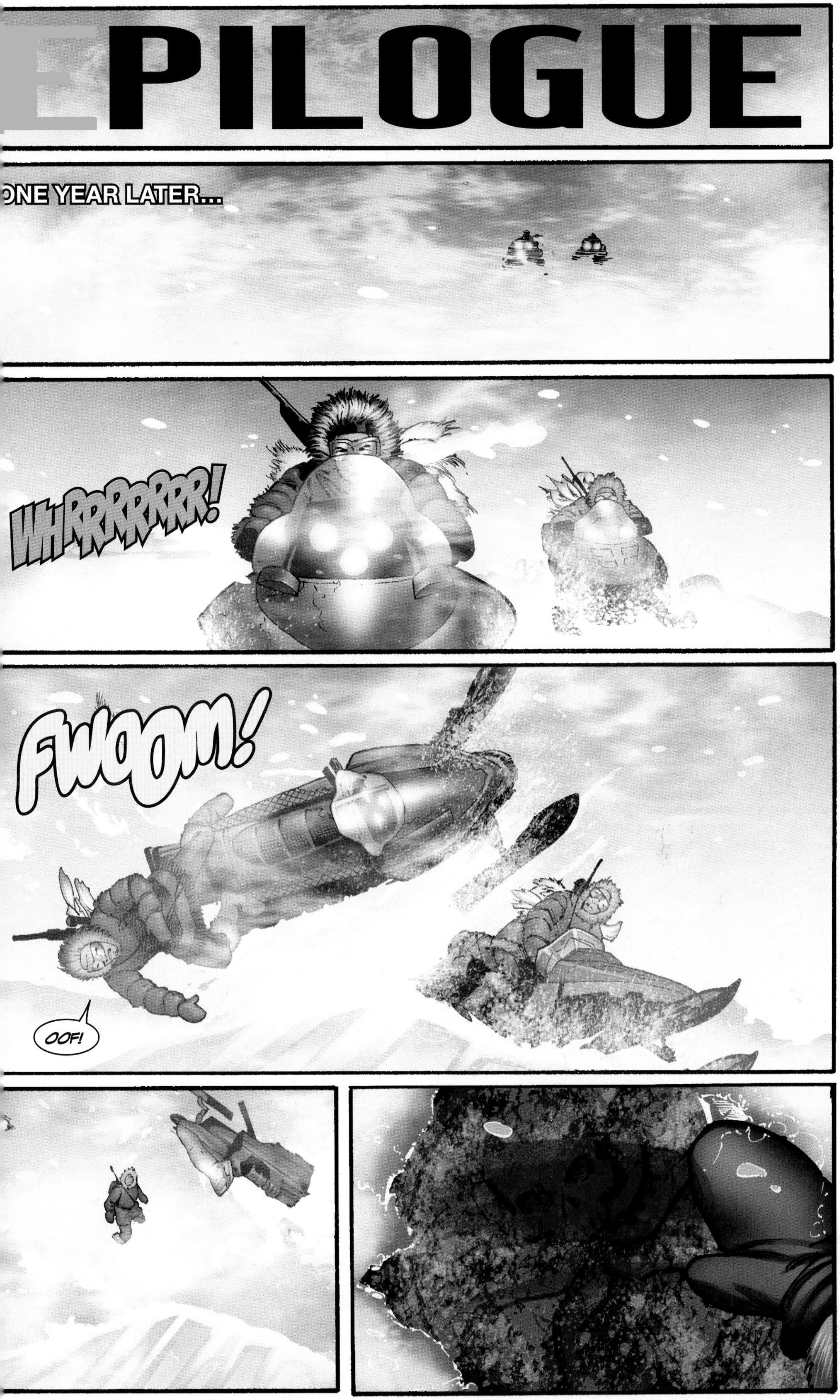
EPILOGUE
ONE YEAR LATER...
WHRRRRRRR!
FWOOM!
OOF!

PHIL COULSON
AGENT OF S.H.I.E.L.D.

DING!

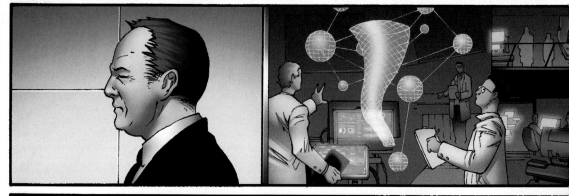

PROJECT
MR. BLUE

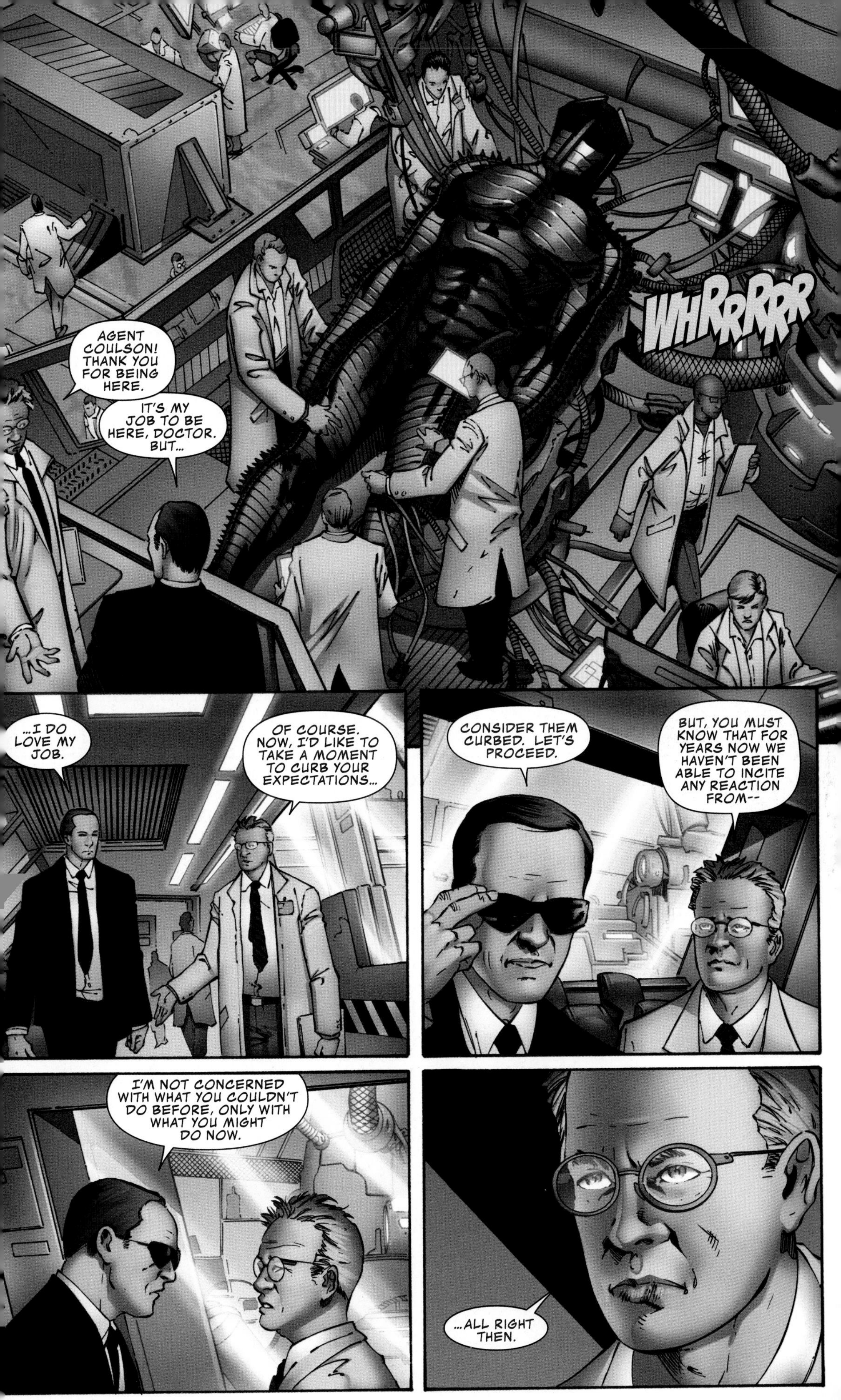

WHRRRRR
AGENT COULSON! THANK YOU FOR BEING HERE.
IT'S MY JOB TO BE HERE, DOCTOR. BUT...
...I DO LOVE MY JOB.
OF COURSE. NOW, I'D LIKE TO TAKE A MOMENT TO CURB YOUR EXPECTATIONS...
CONSIDER THEM CURBED. LET'S PROCEED.
BUT, YOU MUST KNOW THAT FOR YEARS NOW WE HAVEN'T BEEN ABLE TO INCITE ANY REACTION FROM--
I'M NOT CONCERNED WITH WHAT YOU COULDN'T DO BEFORE, ONLY WITH WHAT YOU MIGHT DO NOW.
...ALL RIGHT THEN.

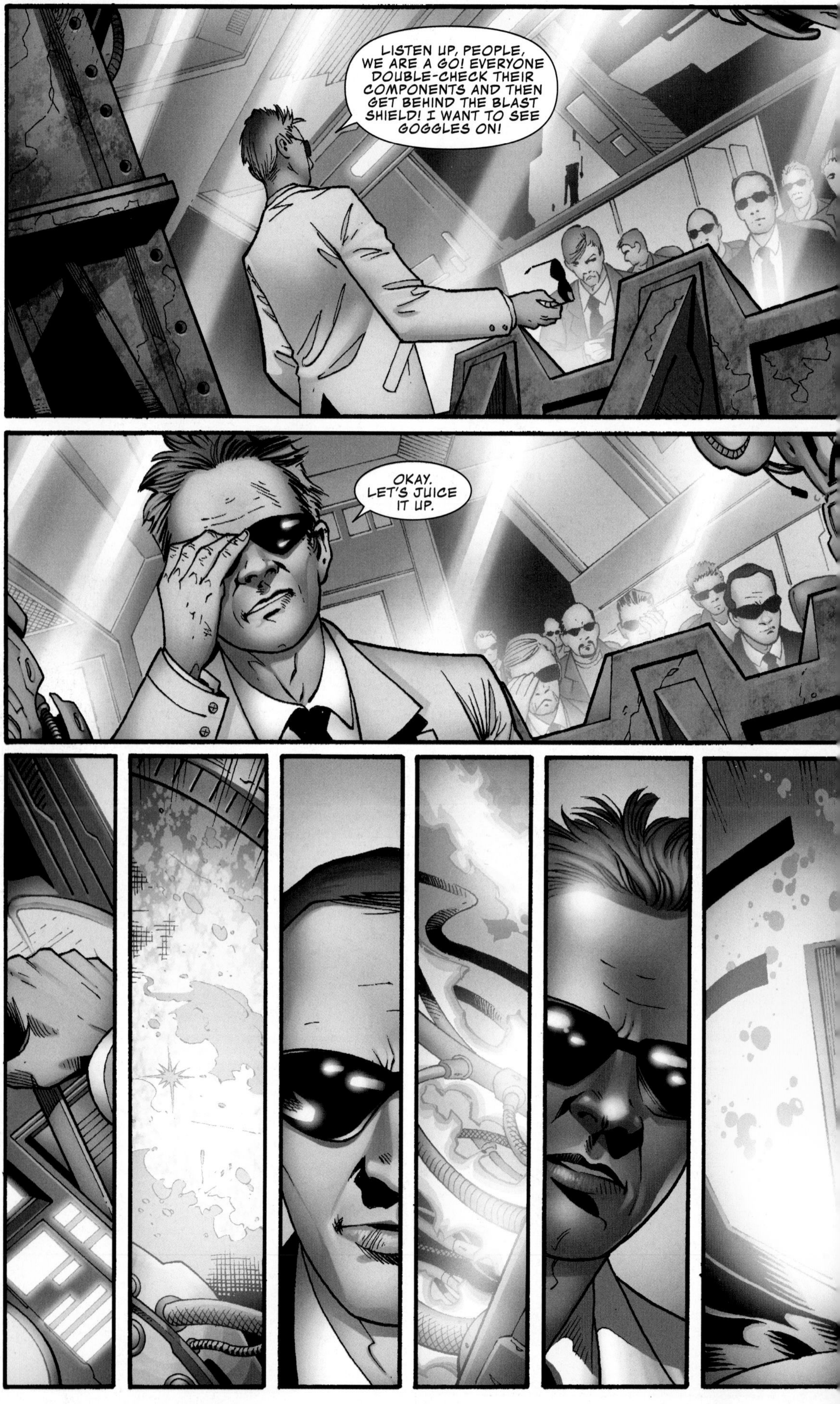
LISTEN UP, PEOPLE, WE ARE A GO! EVERYONE DOUBLE-CHECK THEIR COMPONENTS AND THEN GET BEHIND THE BLAST SHIELD! I WANT TO SEE GOGGLES ON!
OKAY. LET'S JUICE IT UP.

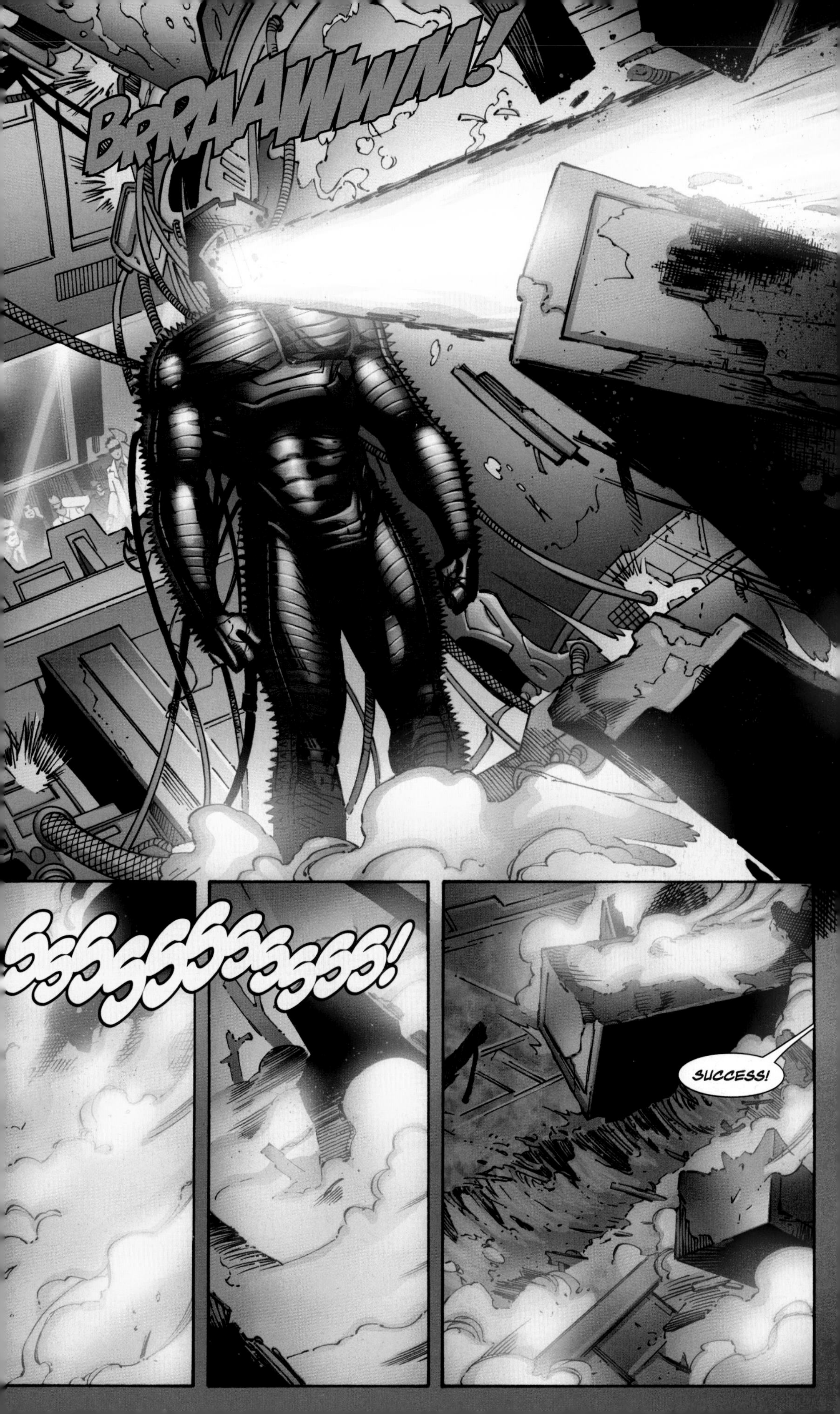
BRRAAWWWM!
SSSSSSSSSSSS!
SUCCESS!

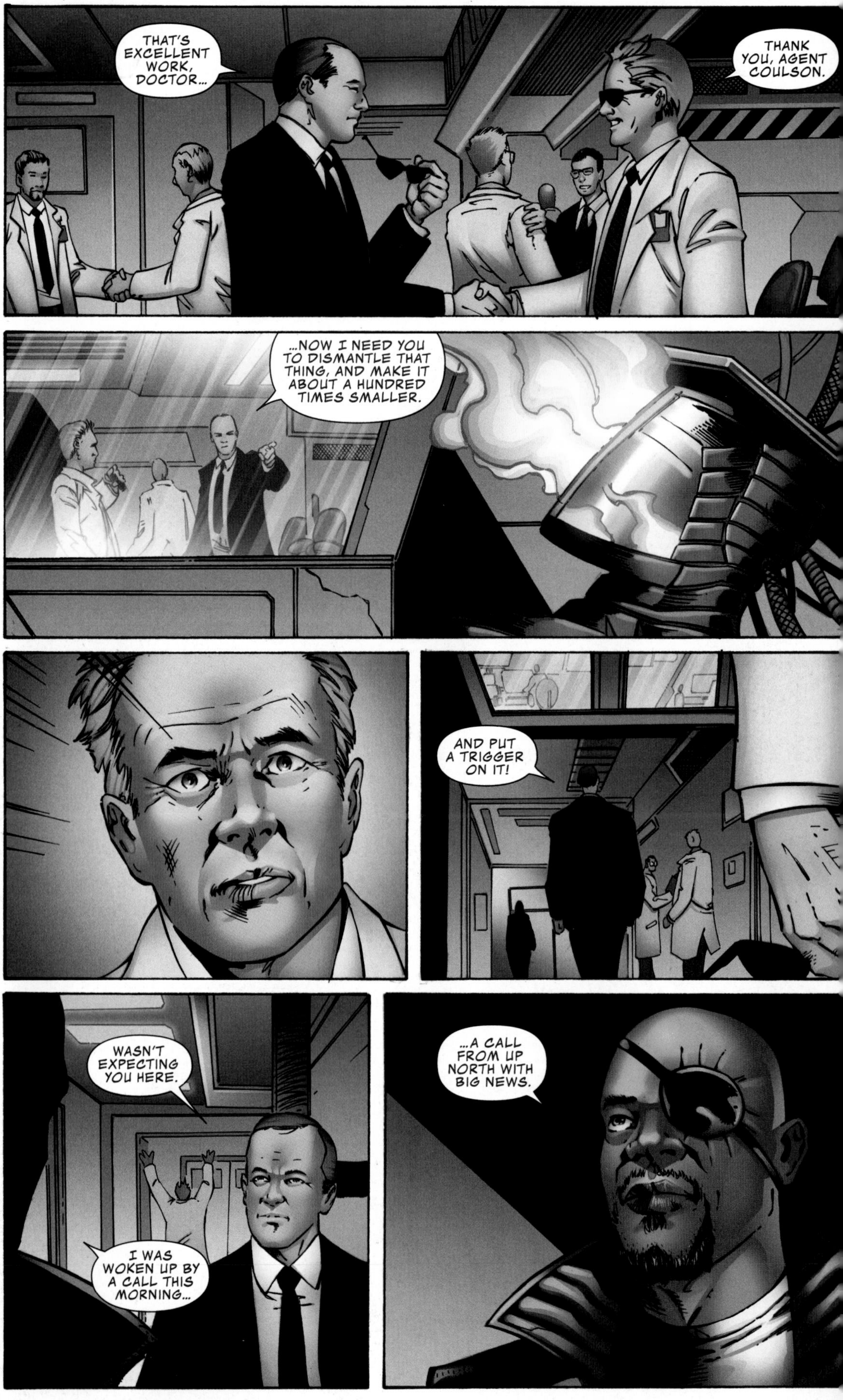
THAT'S EXCELLENT WORK, DOCTOR...
THANK YOU, AGENT COULSON.
...NOW I NEED YOU TO DISMANTLE THAT THING, AND MAKE IT ABOUT A HUNDRED TIMES SMALLER.
AND PUT A TRIGGER ON IT!
WASN'T EXPECTING YOU HERE.
I WAS WOKEN UP BY A CALL THIS MORNING...
...A CALL FROM UP NORTH WITH BIG NEWS.

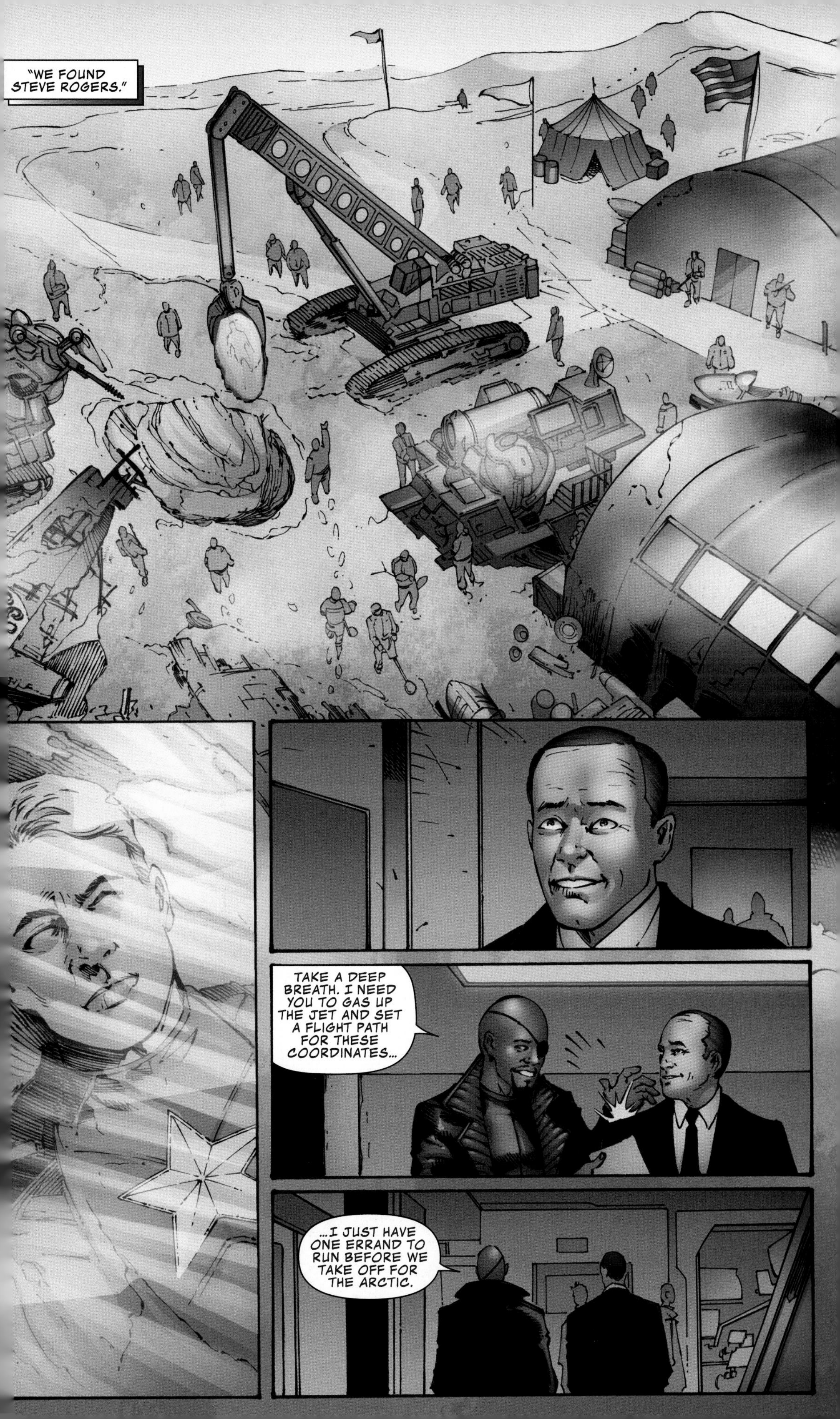
"WE FOUND STEVE ROGERS."
TAKE A DEEP BREATH. I NEED YOU TO GAS UP THE JET AND SET A FLIGHT PATH FOR THESE COORDINATES...
...I JUST HAVE ONE ERRAND TO RUN BEFORE WE TAKE OFF FOR THE ARCTIC.

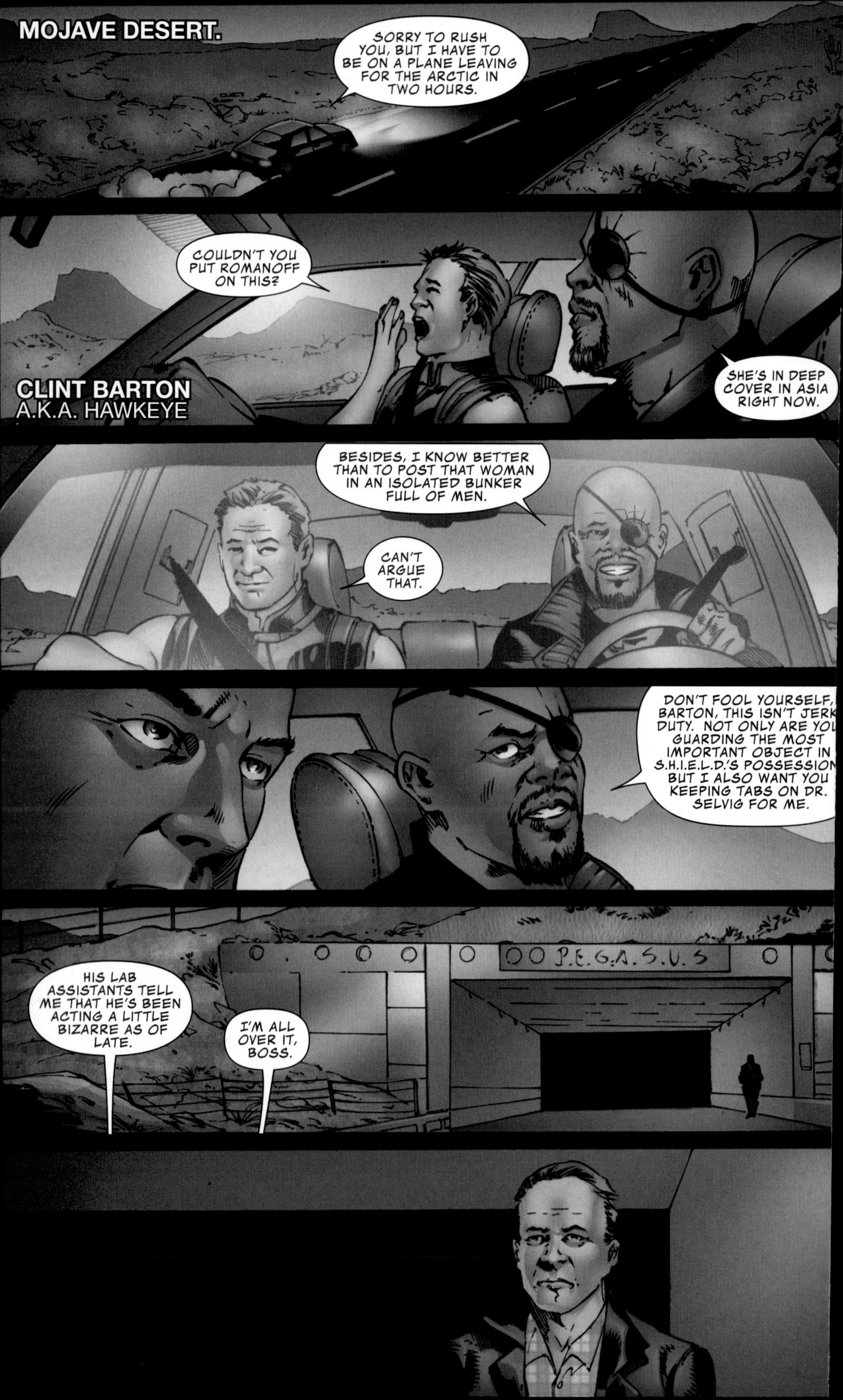
MOJAVE DESERT.
SORRY TO RUSH YOU, BUT I HAVE TO BE ON A PLANE LEAVING FOR THE ARCTIC IN TWO HOURS.
COULDN'T YOU PUT ROMANOFF ON THIS?
CLINT BARTON A.K.A. HAWKEYE
SHE'S IN DEEP COVER IN ASIA RIGHT NOW.
BESIDES, I KNOW BETTER THAN TO POST THAT WOMAN IN AN ISOLATED BUNKER FULL OF MEN.
CAN'T ARGUE THAT.
DON'T FOOL YOURSELF, BARTON, THIS ISN'T JERK DUTY. NOT ONLY ARE YOU GUARDING THE MOST IMPORTANT OBJECT IN S.H.I.E.L.D.'S POSSESSION, BUT I ALSO WANT YOU KEEPING TABS ON DR. SELVIG FOR ME.
P.E.G.A.S.U.S
HIS LAB ASSISTANTS TELL ME THAT HE'S BEEN ACTING A LITTLE BIZARRE AS OF LATE.
I'M ALL OVER IT, BOSS.

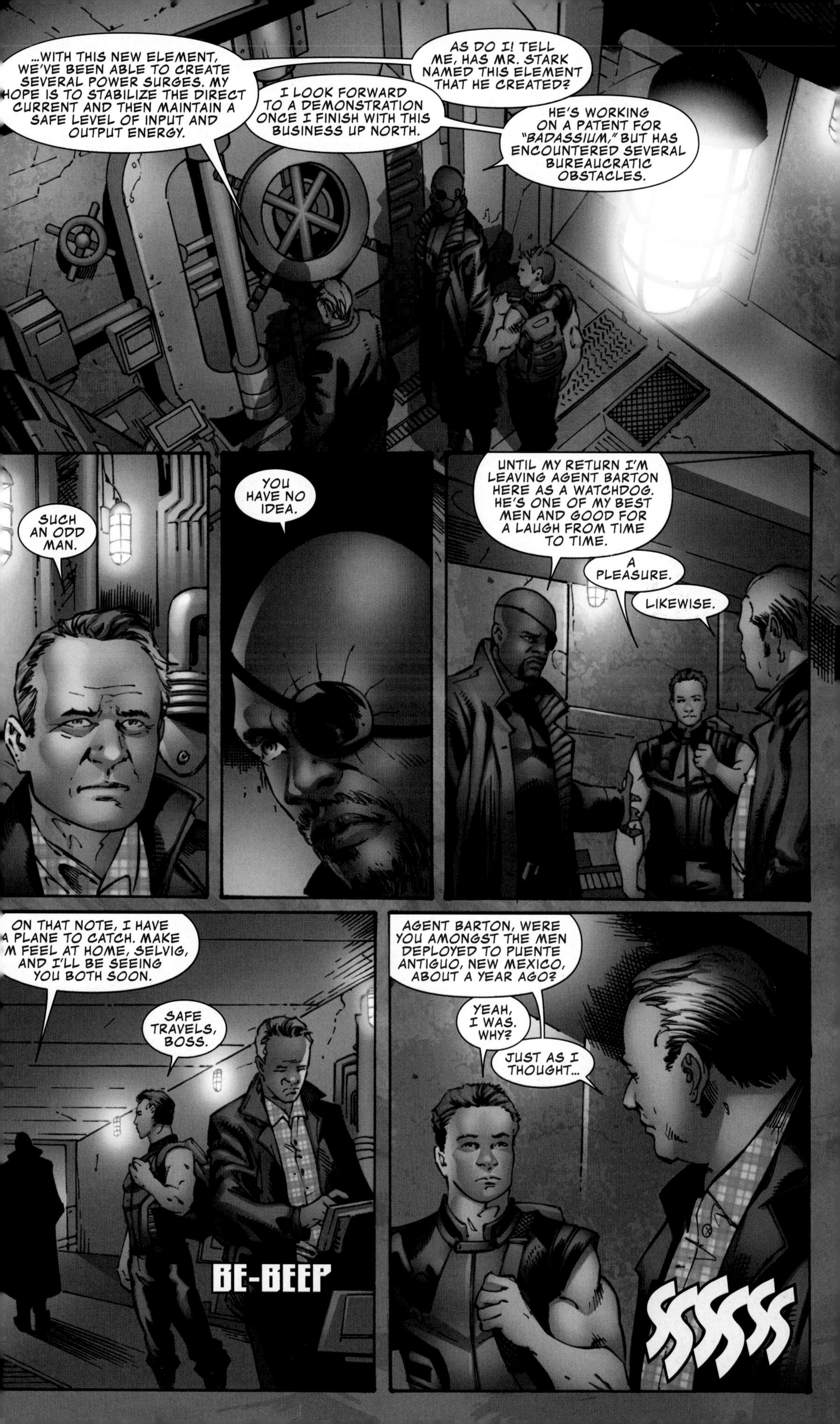
...WITH THIS NEW ELEMENT, WE'VE BEEN ABLE TO CREATE SEVERAL POWER SURGES. MY HOPE IS TO STABILIZE THE DIRECT CURRENT AND THEN MAINTAIN A SAFE LEVEL OF INPUT AND OUTPUT ENERGY.
I LOOK FORWARD TO A DEMONSTRATION ONCE I FINISH WITH THIS BUSINESS UP NORTH.
AS DO I! TELL ME, HAS MR. STARK NAMED THIS ELEMENT THAT HE CREATED?
HE'S WORKING ON A PATENT FOR "BADASSIUM," BUT HAS ENCOUNTERED SEVERAL BUREAUCRATIC OBSTACLES.
SUCH AN ODD MAN.
YOU HAVE NO IDEA.
UNTIL MY RETURN I'M LEAVING AGENT BARTON HERE AS A WATCHDOG. HE'S ONE OF MY BEST MEN AND GOOD FOR A LAUGH FROM TIME TO TIME.
A PLEASURE.
LIKEWISE.
ON THAT NOTE, I HAVE A PLANE TO CATCH. MAKE HIM FEEL AT HOME, SELVIG, AND I'LL BE SEEING YOU BOTH SOON.
SAFE TRAVELS, BOSS.
BE-BEEP
AGENT BARTON, WERE YOU AMONGST THE MEN DEPLOYED TO PUENTE ANTIGUO, NEW MEXICO, ABOUT A YEAR AGO?
YEAH, I WAS. WHY?
JUST AS I THOUGHT...
SSSSS

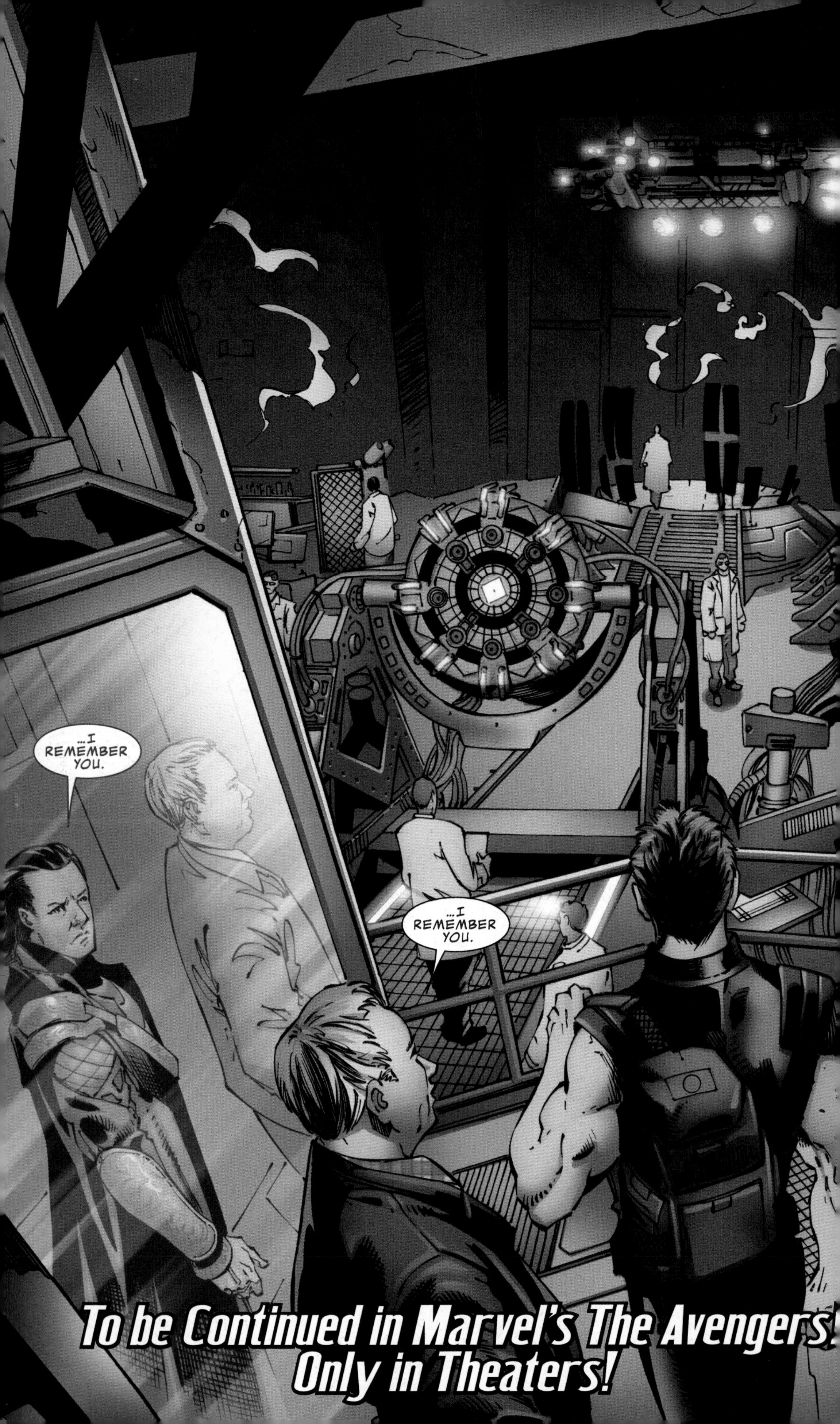
...I REMEMBER YOU.
...I REMEMBER YOU.
To be Continued in Marvel's The Avengers!
Only in Theaters!

THE ADVENTURE CONTINUES IN:

MARVEL

THE AVENGERS

IN THEATERS EVERYWHERE
MAY 4, 2012

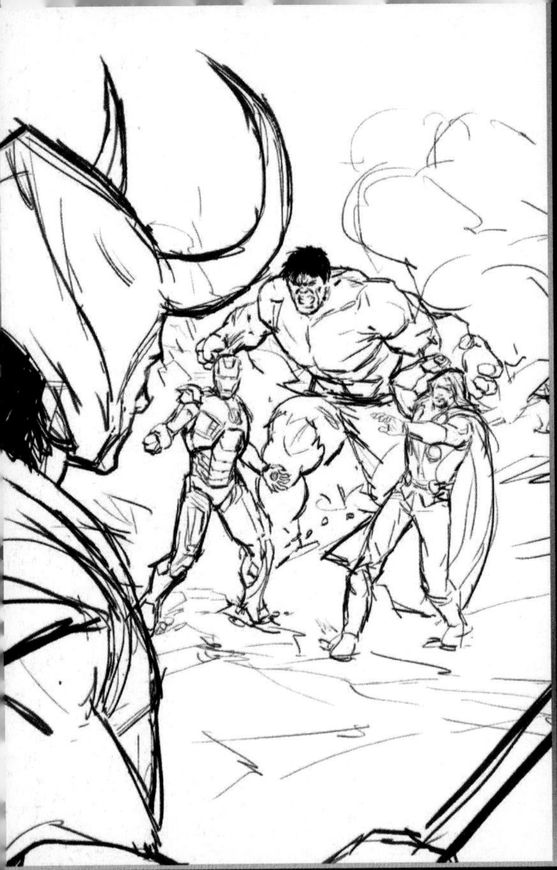
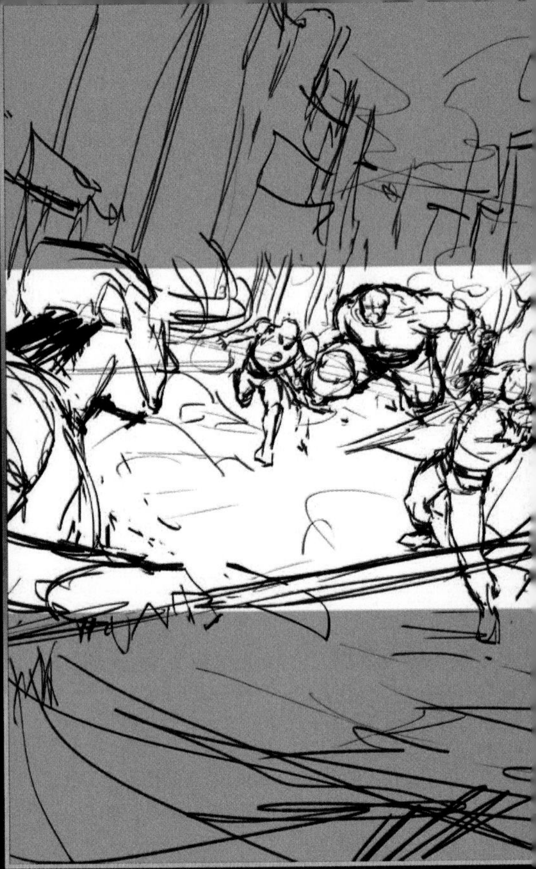
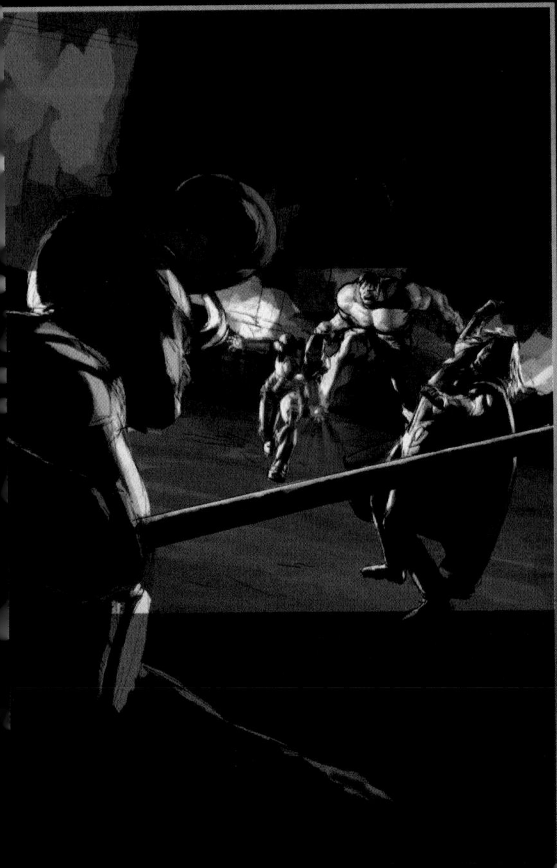
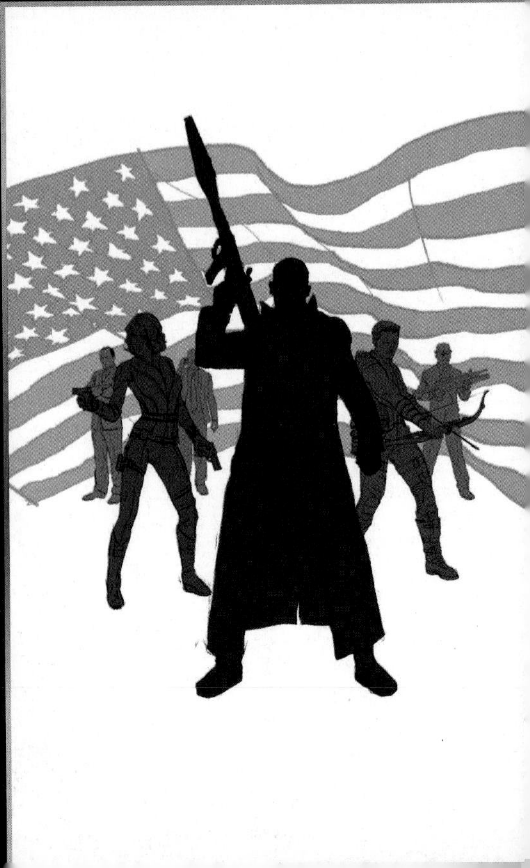

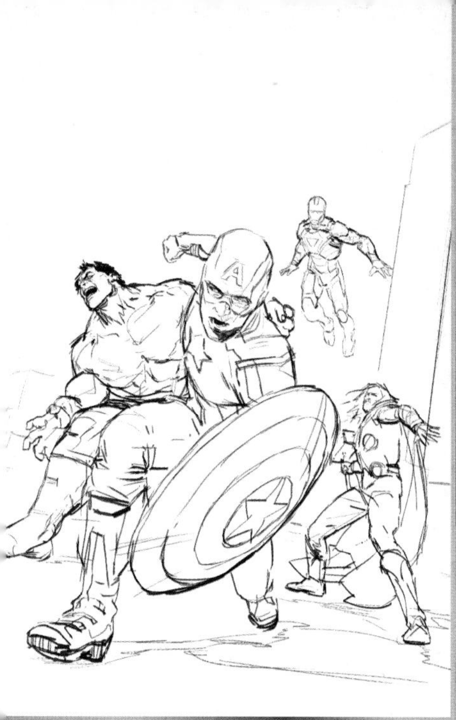
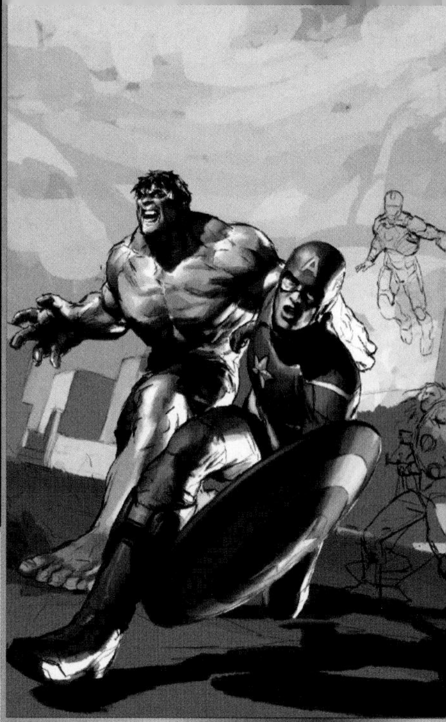
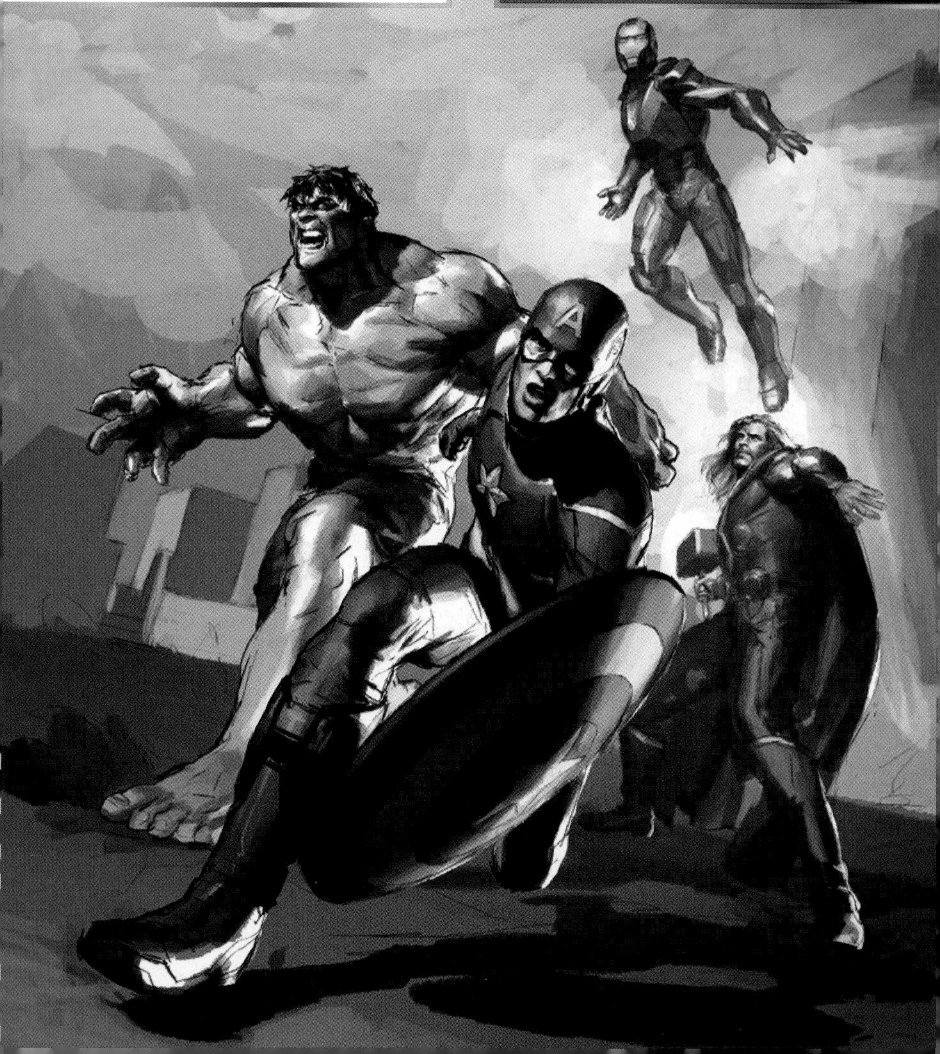

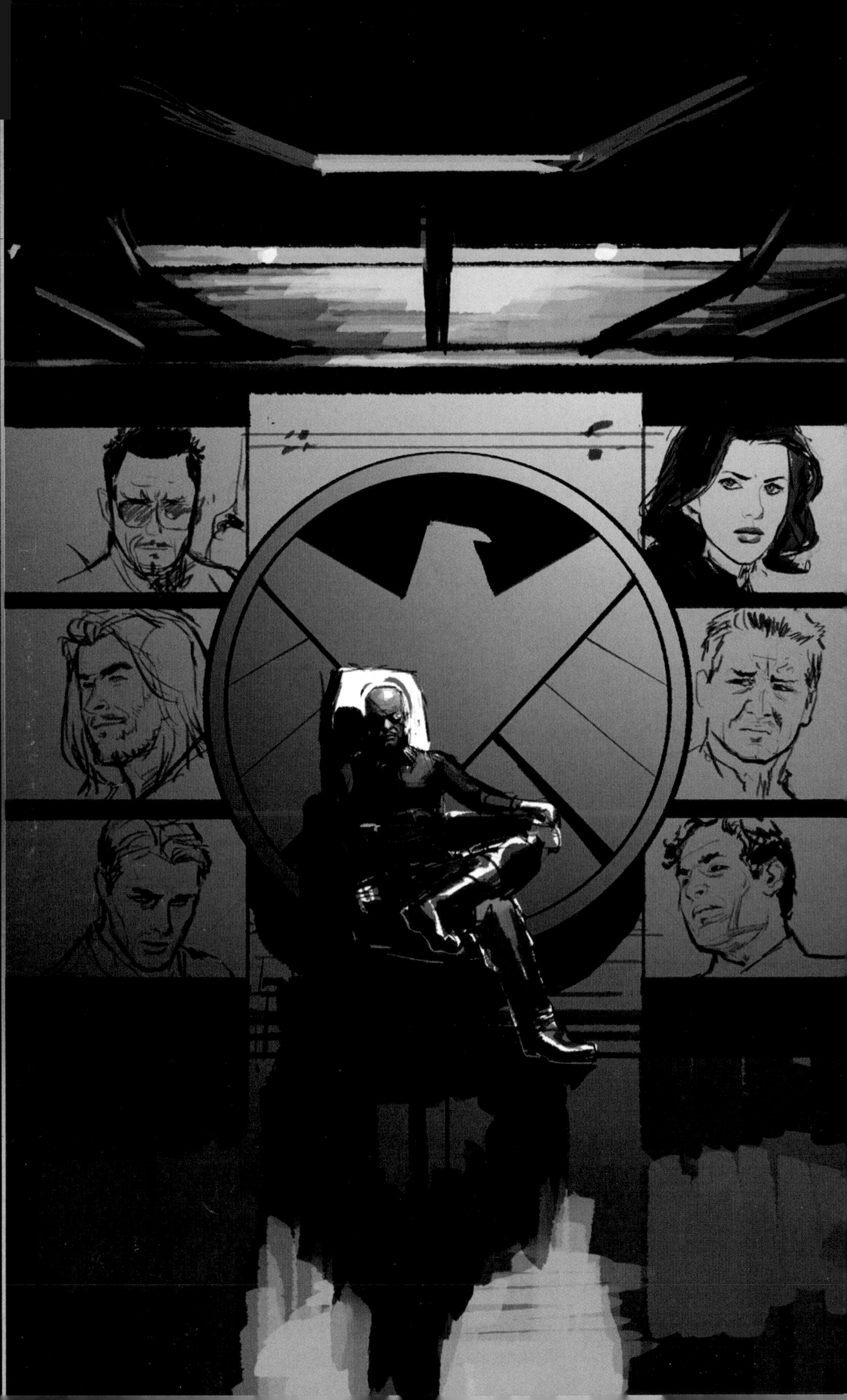